Queerly Cosmopolitan

Timothy Eugene Murphy

Queerly Cosmopolitan

Bohemia and Belonging in a Brazilian Middle-of-Nowhere City

Timothy Eugene Murphy
Worcester State University
Worcester, MA, USA

ISBN 978-3-030-00295-4   ISBN 978-3-030-00296-1   (eBook)
https://doi.org/10.1007/978-3-030-00296-1

Library of Congress Control Number: 2018956171

This Palgrave Pivot imprint is published by the registered company Springer Nature
Switzerland AG
The registered company address is: Gewerbestrasse 11, 6330 Cham, Switzerland

For the galera and all those who wonder where they belong

PREFACE

In a Brazilian city undergoing rapid socioeconomic and cultural change, residents struggle to establish a sense of place and belonging for themselves. When I first came to Teresina in 2003, the population had grown immensely in a short amount of time, and long-standing residents often remarked on the increasing presence of unfamiliar faces in their midst. It had become, by many accounts, a city of strangers. But Teresina was not only growing in population. Perhaps more importantly, its middle class was growing. Residents of Teresina's elite and upwardly mobile neighborhoods often appeared hyperaware of the presence of others in public settings—perhaps hoping to recognize them, to size them up, or to simply take them in. Still, a large segment of the population continued to live quite modestly, often struggling to make ends meet. Citywide power outages were not uncommon at the time and Internet crashes were frequent. It was in this context that I came to know the galera—a tightly knit alternative community of women and men trying to establish a sense of belonging in an expanding world of socially conservative and status-conscious middle-class residents.

By the time I began writing this book in 2016 for undergraduate students in the social sciences, Brazil's economy had undergone both an economic boom and an economic bust, and Teresina's middle class was more prevalent than ever before. Condominium high-rises had multiplied exponentially since 2003, and were no longer solely the domain of elites. Cars regularly flooded the streets at peak hours, resulting in unprecedented traffic jams, and Internet access proliferated with a spike in establishments offering free Wi-Fi. New stores specializing in modern furniture, appliances, and the latest fashions multiplied alongside modern restaurants, cafés, bars, and supermarkets catering to consumers with an increasingly cosmopolitan appetite. The galera had expanded and become more amorphous than ever before, as new alliances formed and other groups of alternative folk and their creative projects gained greater recognition. The once highly restricted norms around people's appearances in spaces of upward mobility had loosened significantly, allowing for a much greater diversity of styles and fashions in virtually all settings. The prevalence of the Internet, and social media in particular, had dramatically altered social life. Quips like, "Now, everyone's a DJ" or "Now everyone's an artist/photographer," referring to the increased availability and use of music, digital technology, and social media, were not uncommon. In addition, the once novel practice of meeting people online through social platforms had become a common occurrence. Several participants in the galera during my research in 2009 and 2010 had relocated to other major cities in Brazil or abroad to continue their education, pursue employment, or simply take advantage of what these distant places offered. Some have remained afar, while others have since returned to Teresina to be closer to their families and to take advantage of the economic security that being closer to family members affords them. Yet the quest to establish a sense of belonging persists for many as the city and its residents continue to transform through increased opportunities for consumption and greater access to distant worlds.

The book is divided into two parts. Part I—"Be-longing"—presents Teresina, Brazil, as a somewhere in the middle of nowhere and members of a rapidly expanding middle class trying to establish a sense of belonging for themselves during a time of acute urbanization. Part II—"Queerly Cosmopolitan"—investigates how a community of bohemians carves out a sense of belonging for itself by following its participants through different realms of life—nocturnal bohemia, work, family, and intimate friendships.

Worcester, MA, USA   Timothy Eugene Murphy

ACKNOWLEDGMENTS

For the completion of this book, I owe a tremendous amount of thanks to numerous people in different places. This project would not have been possible were it not for the many people in Teresina with whom I developed intimate and lasting friendships over the years. Though they shall remain nameless, I would like to express a heartfelt "thank you" to all participants in the galera for their tremendous hospitality, openness, kindness, patience, hours of conversation and laughter and, most importantly, for allowing me to take on the dual role of close friend and researcher in many of their lives. Also in Teresina, I would like to thank my former bosses, coworkers, and friends apart from the galera for their enormous generosity.

A number of grants and fellowships made the research and writing for this book possible: a Doctoral Dissertation Improvement Grant from the National Science Foundation, as well as preliminary research and post-fieldwork writing grants from the Department of Anthropology, the Center for History, Society, and Culture, and the Hemispheric Institute of the Americas at the University of California, Davis.

I would like to thank those in my intellectual community for encouraging and accompanying the development of this project since its initial stages. Donald Donham, Rhacel Parreñas, and Thomas Holloway were all outstanding mentors at UC Davis. I would like to thank Donald Donham for believing in my ability to execute this project from the beginning, for countless discussions about gender and sexuality, and for encouraging me to slow down and question my thinking. I thank Rhacel Parreñas for her continued enthusiasm about this project and for her close attention to my words. I am grateful to Thomas Holloway for sharing his vast knowledge of Brazil with me and for his nuanced reading of my claims and translations.

Numerous people have read, listened, and provided invaluable comments and suggestions during different stages of the project. I would like to thank those affiliated with the Anthropology Department at UC Davis and James Smith, Smriti Srinivas, Li Zhang, Suad Joseph, Carol Smith, Nicholas D'Avella, Ayesha Nibbe, Lena Meari, Rossio Motta, Daniel Mains, Ramah McKay, Sarah Mathis, Chris Krupa, Michelle Stewart, Vivian Choi, Chris Kortright, Leah Wiste, Jake Culbertson, Maya Costa-Pinto, Shaheen Amirebrahimi, Joanne Goodsell, and Jeremy Campbell, in particular. I am especially indebted to my close writing companions— Bascom Guffin, Kari Schroeder, Jonathan Echeverri Zuluaga, Rima Praspaliauskiene, and Madeline Otis Campbell—for their countless readings, insight, conversations, and encouragement over the years. I also would like to thank Brazilian anthropologists Peter Fry, Sérgio Carrara, Patrícia Pinho, and Fabiano Gontijo for their support and encouraging discussions about my project and Alejo Lerzundi for granting me access to the CEPRO Foundation's library in Teresina. I would also like to thank my colleagues at Worcester State University for their encouragement in writing this book.

Friends and family in numerous locations have provided tremendous emotional and intellectual support. I would like to thank Leandro Ramos, Leonardo Ramos, Luana Amaro Muniz, Eduardo Salles, Mateus Araújo, Francisco Xavier, and Luciana Den Júlio for their exceptional hospitality, companionship, and kindness. I am especially thankful to my family—my mom, dad, and Kathleen Hart in particular—for believing in me and encouraging me throughout the whole process. I would also like to thank Jenny Miller, Deganit Nuur, Jeff Root, Dena Ghieth, Hilary Swarts, John Hong, Joe Foley, and Lance Morosini for their love and support. Finally, a very special thanks goes to Krista Chael for helping me document my research in Teresina and for providing illustrations for the book.

CONTENTS

LIST OF FIGURES

PART I

Be-longing

CHAPTER 1

A Middle-of-Nowhere Somewhere

Abstract The chapter begins with a story detailing the ethnographer's initial encounter with a community of bohemians on which the ethnography centers. It then reveals the problem underpinning the entire book: Teresina, Brazil's location in the poorest state in the nation's poorest region, renders it marginal at best within the national imaginary. When Teresina's population growth is met with economic prosperity, status performances among the city's large and expanding middle class seem to only exacerbate residents' desires to establish a sense of place and belonging. The chapter introduces the book's concept of *be-longing in the world at home*—being both local and cosmopolitan in a city like Teresina. The chapter concludes with explanations about fieldwork, questions of representation, and the structure of the book.

Keywords Belonging • Urbanization • Cities • Brazil

When I started teaching at the foreign-language school in the mall, I must have walked past the Levi's store on five different occasions, waving back at Henrique and his friends until amid a good amount of chuckling, they started exaggerating their gestures and yelling, "*Vem cá! Vem cá!*" ("Come here! Come here!"). With some hesitation, I entered the tiny clothing store. Between my broken Portuguese and their limited English, we arrived at the heart of the misunderstanding: an opening and closing fist

© The Author(s) 2019
T. E. Murphy, *Queerly Cosmopolitan*,
https://doi.org/10.1007/978-3-030-00296-1_1

Fig. 1.1   *Teresomewhere*, by Krista Chael 2009

with the palm facing out signifies "come here" for most Brazilians, while for me, it meant nothing more than a cordial, if childlike, wave of hello. Red with embarrassment and feeling flustered, I did my best to nod, smile, and supply them with a "*legal!*" ("cool!") or two. Henrique, who I had met just a few weeks earlier on my way into the mall, smiled and handed me a black flyer covered in neon script with the word "INFINITY" written in big white Atari 2600-style letters across the top.

Around 11 o'clock the following Saturday night, Henrique and his friend Mariel picked me up to go to Infinity: a rave. After no more than ten minutes of trying to keep up with their conversation, I watched Mariel pull into a parking spot in front of a worn-down apartment complex on the corner of a busy intersection. As we climbed a set of stairs, Henrique asked me if I liked *cerveja* (beer). "*Claro!*" ("Of course!") I replied, feeling thirsty and still unaccustomed to Teresina's incessant heat. Mariel pulled out some keys and opened a door. "You are welcome. My house," Mariel said in English with a chuckle of uncertainty about her execution. She flipped on a light switch and directed us into her glowing ultraviolet living room complete with fluorescent posters, a few neon dream catchers, and fluffy floor cushions. Henrique promptly kicked off his flip-flops and offered me a cigarette as Mariel disappeared into the kitchen. By the time she returned with a tray of beers, Henrique had managed to put on a CD and explain that we would spend some time hanging out at Mariel's before going to the rave. After chatting about the eccentricities of Mariel's apartment, trying to locate ourselves in relation to the rest of the city from her living room window, and listening to a diverse selection of music, it was after one in the morning. "*Bora?*" ("Shall we go?"), said Mariel.

The drive took us back in the direction of my apartment and then onward to the outskirts of the city. Within a matter of minutes, there were no longer any stop signs or street lights or roundabouts, only gravelly roads of dusty ochre and denser patches of what looked like giant-sized ferns jutting up out of the earth. Once we turned down the dark forest lane, parked cars lining both sides signaled we had arrived. A dark-skinned, slender, older-looking man in tattered clothes and flip-flops walked into the dusty beams of our headlights. He motioned us past him, pointing to a spot a bit further down the lane. Once we were parked, we began walking toward a light hanging on a brick wall near a small crowd of people. Henrique led us through the opening in the wall past a stocky security guard dressed in black. After presenting our tickets, Mariel motioned for us to follow her as she headed into the dark, candle-lit labyrinth of sandy soil, twisted trees, and the sound of quick drumbeats playing in the distance.

Infinity was quite similar to a number of other *festas* (parties)[1] hosted by this particular community back in 2003. They often took place a good distance from downtown and the East Zone on the property of a country house. The number of attendees would range anywhere from 200 to 500. Festa producers would use their contacts to find someone willing to rent a weekend home for a small fee. During the festa, the house would remain locked up, and the producers would transform the grounds with creative applications of dim lights, stretched Lycra, beanbag chairs and a number of other borrowed and rented decorations, from glow-in-the-dark stream-

---

[1] In Brazilian Portuguese, "festa" means "party," and in this particular case, "rave."

ers to psychedelic posters of Hindu deities, all in the attempt to create a handful of distinct environments—a dance floor, a beanbag lounge for relaxing or making out, and an area reserved for food and drink. The dance floor, always ruled by a deejay—usually from Teresina but occasionally from some larger, more well-known city, like Fortaleza or Rio de Janeiro, would be marked by a clear open space made of grass, concrete, or bare earth in front of the turntables.

Throughout the night and into the morning, deejays would play mostly electronic music, specifically, Trance and House. Beneath lofty crown-shaped babaçu palms and a glittered black sky, lone bodies moving in harmony to the beats of the music would populate the dance floor. Often with closed eyes, whether sober, drunk, stoned, or tripping, people would bounce, swing, float, twist, and jump, losing themselves in the moment. At times, they would find themselves watching one another, engaging in a spontaneous dialogue with their movements, often accompanied by smiles and laughter. In the other environments and in the dark spots between them, friends would chat and couples and strangers would cruise, flirt, and make out with same-sex and opposite-sex partners.

As the early-rising equatorial sun started to lighten the sky and the festa began to wind down, Henrique, Mariel, and I found ourselves among about two dozen people gathered a ways away from the action on a large concrete patio near a swimming pool. Most everyone convened there seemed to know one another as they sat talking to one another and sharing their last beers, joints, and cigarettes. Raquel, the producer, sat barefoot cradled in her girlfriend's arms, talking to one of the deejays who was standing with a CD case in one hand and his girlfriend's hand in the other. A shirtless man named Bruno in linen pants kicked his feet up into a handstand for his friend Sérgio to catch and the two began to walk around the perimeter of the pool laughing. When one girl yelled, "Hey, where is João?," a lanky man with glitter in his short curly hair responded in a highly affected and effeminate manner, "I think he found himself a macho man, sweetie," inciting a brief roar of laughter.

From that moment onward, I would develop close relationships with a number of these people and become increasingly more incorporated into their *galera* (clique)—a continually fluctuating community of no less than 200 people with whom I have engaged on and off over the course of 15 years. Though a fair amount about the galera has changed since I first came to know it in 2003, the sketch above touches on much that remains at its core: a shared desire for and participation in unconventional experiences and sensations via novel types of social events, ambiances, music, design, art, and performances. A community centered on avant-garde esthetics, cultural appropriations of distant worlds, and experimentation, the galera carves out a space in which numerous unorthodox approaches to community, placemaking, belonging, gender, and sexuality are encouraged to flourish. A queer form of belonging, indeed.

SOMEWHERE NOWHERE

When preparing to move to Teresina to teach English in 2003, there was little available on Teresina at the university library in the city where I was living—only a few scientific studies about things like ground water and tropical diseases. There was even less available online—no Wikipedia pages, no YouTube videos, no online newspapers, no climate indices, only a few photographs. I distinctly remember one of a colonial-style building lit up at night and another of a few people involved in a fashion show at a local shopping mall. With such a dearth of information available on the city, I decided I would have to trust the description I got from the American who lined me up with the job there: Teresina's population was around one million, the city was hot, far from the beach, and now home to a McDonald's.

Though somewhat helpful, this was still an incredibly limited amount of information to have before moving to a place—a fact that is glaringly apparent to me today when I consider the wealth of details about Teresina a person now could obtain by taking even a cursory glance at a resident's Instagram or Twitter feed. After about one month of preparing to move and nearly 24 hours in transit after departing Chicago's O'Hare Airport, I was on my final descent into this place about which I knew so very little. There were only four of us on that TAM airbus—two Catholic nuns, a stout Brazilian man, and myself—the smallest number of passengers I would ever see on such a flight over the years to come. As the plane descended, I stared out the window, intrigued by the vibrant textures and colors of the dense patches of palm tree forest and orange-colored soil. Just before touching down, I caught a glimpse of two young shirtless boys playing soccer on a dirt road. For me, this was the final confirmation—no matter how cliché—that I was on the verge of encountering this place I had been trying so hard to imagine.

This, I thought to myself, is Brazil.

*   *   *

Teresina is the capital of the northeastern state of Piauí. Situated in the heart of Brazil's poorest region, Piauí is one of the country's poorest states (Lima 2003), continually wracked by drought in the South and evidencing extreme inequality in all directions. Over the past 60 years, Teresina has experienced a tremendous amount of population growth due to rural-urban migration. With approximately 90,000 residents in 1950 (Nascimento 2007), today the city is home to well over 800,000 people (IBGE 2017). Although Teresina has been hard-pressed to adequately absorb such considerable growth, Brazil's economic boom and new socio-economic policies have dramatically altered the look and feel of this sizzling equatorial city. Having spent roughly three years on and off there during the administration of former president Luiz Inácio "Lula" da Silva (2003–2010), I witnessed a number of significant changes in Teresina's landscape: dozens of ultramodern towering condominiums popping up around the city's only two shopping malls; car dealerships racking up some of the highest numbers of sales in the country as cars began flooding the streets; residents who not so long ago went to the shopping malls only to cool off began standing in lines to purchase all kinds of appliances—from washing machines to laptops to plasma TVs; and flights in and out of Teresina that were sparsely populated in 2003 became increasingly packed, with at least a handful of first-time flyers always on board.

Changes like those I witnessed in Teresina are representative of a broader trend taking place throughout Brazil. The Brazilian middle class, which is defined in terms of new official national standards as well as by lifestyle and self-identification,[2] is bigger than ever and feels as ambiguous of a category as in the US; it includes people ranging from maids who ride buses and sell Avon, to civil servants, doctors, and small business owners who own more than one car, have second homes in the countryside, and send their children to prestigious private schools. In Teresina, all of this change has brought with it a great amount of uncertainty about one's place in the world.

With residents' increased access to consumption, it is becoming less and less obvious who is truly *chique*—meaning sophisticated, wealthy, and powerful—and who is just faking it, causing some to doubt their own ability to pass as authentically chique. Because being chique partly depends on

---

[2] In Chap. 3, I explain Brazil's new official national standards for class. For discussions of middle classes as defined by lifestyle and self-identification, see, for example, Fernandes 2006; Bettie 2003; Heiman et al. 2012.

one's ability to approximate and appropriate *"fora"* (a term that often signals a particular set of foreign places and cultures imagined to be superior), all kinds of foreign imports and imitation foreign imports   from words to cars to fashions to electronics—are wreaking havoc on Teresina's economy of chique. As a result, while a good portion of the middle class is being afforded unprecedented opportunities to distance and distinguish themselves from the "popular"/lower classes, for others, performing chique is becoming increasingly more difficult to pull off.

In large part due to greater access to credit, exposure to media, and increased opportunities for travel, many Teresinenses are beginning to see themselves less in terms of the countryside hometowns from which they hail or their immediate neighbors in Teresina, and more in terms of their entire city. People seek recognition by trying to move into the chique-est neighborhoods, attend the chique-est social events, and be seen sporting the chique-est fashions. In other moments, members of Teresina's broad middle class increasingly understand themselves in terms of larger geographic spheres of region, nation, and world. For example, not long after first arriving in Teresina in 2003 to teach English in the mall, I was surprised to hear my students, and later other Teresinenses, tell me a number of widely circulated stories about their state and city that conveyed their lack of resources, culture, and importance.

By the time my one-year contract at the language school was up, I had far more questions about this northeastern Brazilian city than when I first arrived. I couldn't help but wonder what it means to call a place like Teresina "home"—to live in a place in which, on the one hand, the world has seemed to have landed in one's backyard overnight, and on the other, the abundance of knowledge suddenly available conjures up peoples and places that are only slightly easier to reach physically. What is it like to be regularly faced with a discourse of inferiority about one's city; to be part of an expanding social stratum in which one's social position is at best unclear and at worst under constant threat; and, as a participant in the galera, to continually take refuge in an alternative community of bohemians in such a place?

*   *   *

I write this book from the position that although the experience of living in Teresina is unique, its contours are far more widespread than many of us would like to think. Teresina is not just another out-of-the-way location where an anthropologist has found a peculiar phenomenon worthy of an ethnographic study. Rather, Teresina represents a particular *kind* of place—a place that, while substantial in size, is thought by many to lie somewhere between unimportant and "the middle of nowhere."

Gregory Clancey's (2004) claim that "the 'out-of-the-way' may indeed be an urban legend unconsciously sustained by our focus on a hierarchal urban network of globe-spanning proportions" (2004: 2335) is a salient one. In a world whose population is estimated to have surpassed seven billion, cities that do not fall among the most populous or the most culturally and economically influential are often talked about as if they are not only insignificant, but also rare. It is as if we imagine a world in which the majority of humans grow up and live in the so-called important places and that far fewer claim home to a number of inconsequential elsewheres. While the so-called primate cities (Jefferson 1939) still stand out in sharp contrast to other cities in some countries in terms of both population and national influence, a number of other countries evidence numerous regional hubs with large and growing populations—emerging economies like Brazil, India, and China are cases in point. In light of the fact that most urban residents in the world live in cities in which the population does not exceed 500,000 and that two-thirds of urban residents in the developing world live in cities of less than one million people (Clancey 2004: 2337), Clancey argues that the concept of "world cities" conflates "the largest urban centres into a single networked largeness which leaves the rest of the world arguably smaller and more remote" (2004: 2337). While Clancey's assertion may partly explain why the most populous and globally influential cities of the world receive such a disproportionate amount attention in both popular and scholarly discourse, the problem remains: although the majority of people in the world reside (or are likely to have resided) in a "not-so-important" place, more than a few seem to be somewhat reluctant to acknowledge this fact.

Many of us continue to operate with the long-standing notion that where a person is from and/or resides amounts to the type of person that she is; that the so-called cosmopolitans are from the so-called cosmopolitan places and vice versa. Yet many people who live in such places know better. Certainly not all, but a fair number of people who relocate to major cities of the world do so in order to take advantage of their diverse options for leisure and culture (e.g., art, food, museums, shopping, nightlife, and subcultures). In other words, these people's cosmopolitan orientation did not begin in the big city; it began elsewhere and, perhaps, even an "inconsequential" middle of nowhere.

Somewhat surprisingly, the academy has been just as guilty of overlooking this middle, if not "ordinary," category of urban life (Amin and Graham 1997; Robinson 2006). Much scholarship on globalization has focused on wealthy "global cities" (e.g., Friedmann 1986; Sassen 1991) and poor mega cities (e.g., Davis 2006), and attempts to offer a different perspective tend to look to small and/or extremely impoverished communities (e.g., Besnier 2009; Scheper-Hughes 1992; Gregory 2007). Urban studies on Latin America (e.g., Koonings and Kruijt 2007) and in Brazil also tend to focus on major political, economic, and cultural hubs (e.g., Holston 1989; Caldeira 2001; O'Dougherty 2002; Green 2000; Velho 2002; Gontijo 2009; Kulick 1998; McCallum 2005). While a small number of scholars have endeavored to study life in such middle-sized cities in various parts of the world (e.g., Simone 2004; Lamonte 1992; Weiss 2002), few have considered the relationship between the stigmas that can be attached to such places and life there (though see Zhang 2006; Clancey 2004). Following the "ordinary city" approach (Amin and Graham 1997; Robinson 2006), then, this book contributes to efforts to divorce "modernity" from its conventional connotations of "Western," "wealthy," and "major." Especially during this historical moment of acute de-agrarianization and urban growth throughout the developing world and Latin America in particular (Montgomery 2008), coupled with the glaring cultural and political divide between urban and rural populations in the West and much of the globe, this book offers a timely contribution by providing an in-depth study of life in an increasingly relevant category of city in an emerging economy caught in the traffic of global flows.

BE-LONGING IN THE WORLD AT HOME

What follows is a story of place and belonging. It is about the place one imagines oneself to reside in and other places that one imagines exist beyond that place. It is also about the place(s) one imagines oneself to be from and other places to which one imagines oneself to be headed. On the one hand, this story tells of a people's identification with and attachment to a city. On the other hand, it tells of a people's lack of identification and dissatisfaction with that city and the ways they are driven to construct a different kind of place there, sometimes for the enjoyment of others, but more importantly for themselves. This story traces the relationship between where one resides and the life that one builds—and indeed dreams of building—while living there. As such, this is a different kind of story about the experience of being cosmopolitan—one that is embroiled in the daily life of a particular place; one that is technologically and imaginatively mediated and enhanced; and one that is constructed around a thirst for approximating a specific brand of novel and "outside" ways of life. It is also a different story about the experience of being bohemian—one that is fragmented; one that is queer; and one that persists through complex, if not contradictory, relationships to an expanding middle class. It is a story of how cosmopolitan and bohemian subjectivities emerge in a contemporary middle-of-nowhere city.

What follows is a story of what I call *be-longing in the world at home*. "Be-longing" is the experience of longing that takes place when one attempts to secure a rightful place for oneself both in the "world" and at "home." Be-longing is a state of being wrapped in a desire to belong. Longing to belong on various registers, outsiders are this story's focus. From residents of a forgotten place relegated to the margins of the globe (Chap. 2) to people striving daily for recognition within the context of the city's expanding middle class (Chap. 3), to the cultivation of a nocturnal bohemia (Chap. 4), to black sheep maintaining a legitimate place in the milieux of family and work (Chap. 5), to negotiating subjectivities of same-sex desire via intimate friendships (Chap. 6), each chapter of this book addresses outside-ness and the problem of be-longing from a different angle. *Be-longing in the world at home* can mean to desire, to approximate, to harness, and to be a part of worlds that one is unable to reach from where one resides. It can also refer to the experience of never fully realizing one's place where one resides despite enjoying a sense of belonging in distant worlds. At its base, then, this is a story about the desire to belong both in the world and at home—a wish to claim an authentic place in both.

*   *   *

Cosmopolitanism—the notion of global belonging—is one way to understand the proliferating trend for Teresinenses to invoke and appropriate distant and foreign ways of life and aesthetics. Over the last two decades especially, the surge of processes of globalization has sparked considerable scholarly debate about cosmopolitanism (e.g., Breckenridge et al. 2002; Cheah and Robbins 1998). Given the accelerated rate with which people, capital, things, ideas, and simulacra traverse nearly every type of border, notions of belonging are becoming increasingly ambiguous, and such effects of globalization have made reevaluating nationalism, culture, and, thus, cosmopolitanism, imperative. From the Stoics (Malcomson 1998) to Kant (Cheah 1998; Linklater 1999) to the cosmopolitan-as-world-traveler (Robbins 1998; Rapport and Stade 2007), the figure of the cosmopolitan has become a subject of renewed interest for social theorists. While some scholars have argued that cosmopolitan affinities are necessarily post- or antinationalist (Appadurai and Breckenridge 1988; Rée 1998) or antithetical to the local (Hannerz 1990), others have asserted that the national/local is constitutive of and/or benefited by cosmopolitan orientations (Wood 1998; Hall 2003; Dharwadker 2001). It is from this latter position that this book's discussion of *be-longing in the world at home* builds.

Other recent theorizations have radically upset conventional notions of cosmopolitanism by applying a subaltern approach to the concept. For example, an interest in "non-Western" cosmopolitanisms (e.g., Breckenridge et al. 2002) has produced a growing literature (Appiah 1998; Ong 1998; Diouf 2002; Schein 1998). Additionally, people whose cosmopolitan orientations do not depend on the experience of global travel have also been the focus of recent discussions (Pollock 2002; Abbas 2002; Novak 2010), though empirically rich ethnographic studies of such phenomena are still recent and tend to be limited to major cities with high influxes of global capital (Condry 2001) and/or immigrants and tourists (Scheld 2007; Potuoglu-Cook 2006; Wilson 2004). What these studies and others have revealed is the extent to which other-world aesthetics, ideas, practices, and politics become appropriated via technology and the imagination and forge cosmopolitan subjectivities and communities be they national or transnational (Anderson 1983; Appadurai 1996; Chan 2006; Fischer 2010; Parker 1999a; Boellstorff 2005; Manalansan 2003). Still others have considered how a cosmopolitan aesthetics in particular can translate into recognition and status at the level of the local (Wilson 2004; Scheld 2007; Liechty 2003; Calhoun 2008). This book builds from this scholarship by examining cosmopolitan belonging that takes shape not so much through the experience of global travel but rather the imagination, the appropriation of distant lifeways, and the production of novel aesthetics in a growing provincial city at the margins of the globe.

*   *   *

The people I spent the most time interacting with and studying in Teresina—a community of no fewer than 200 men and women invested in

creating an alternative existence largely centered on aesthetically innova-
tive social events in Teresina—do not have a name for their collective.
Instead, they loosely refer to their community as the "*galera*" ("clique").
Given the galera's vast knowledge about and appropriation of aesthetics
associated with other peoples and places, at first glance, it might seem that
the recent literature about how the circulation of media, fashions, and
music (Novak 2010; Fischer 2010; Scheld 2007; Condry 2001) in the
creation of cosmopolitan subjects would encompass the galera's orientation and lifestyle. In a number of ways, the galera is, without a doubt,
cosmopolitan, though of a different ilk from that of Teresina's upwardly
mobile masses. The galera strives less to establish belonging within mainstream society than it does to see itself as nonnormative, bohemian, and
avant-garde. Such an alternative orientation certainly has cosmopolitan
underpinnings, but the galera desires more than to approximate outside
worlds imagined to be superior. It also desires cultural innovation, novel
experiences, and to create an existence in Teresina that radically differs
from that which already exists there. More than simply wanting to harness
all things foreign, participants in the galera are drawn to the strange and
the avant-garde and strive to partake in what is happening on the edge of
the future. Rather than aspiring to be just like some other place or people,
the galera's mission is to create a unique, alternative, and avant-garde existence both *in the world* and *at home*.

What largely sets the galera's cosmopolitan belonging apart from that
of the upwardly mobile masses is what I identify as a shared ethos of queerness. By "queerness," I am not referring to the popular use of "queer" as
an umbrella term for the LGBT community. Instead, the galera's ethos of
queerness refers, in one sense, to identifications with alternative and nonnormative ways of life existing at the margins of mainstream society. For
example, the galera's events, by and large, take place "off-the-grid" of
Teresina's social life, and many have names that either conceal the nature
of the event or reinforce a shared ethos of an alternative and oppositional
stance with respect to Teresina's expanding middle class. Attendees of the
galera's events are often encouraged to experiment with the unconventional by participating in a number of activities: testing their skills as deejays, listening to unfamiliar music, moving their bodies in new ways, and
engaging in unconventional perceptions, affections, and self presentations.
Regarded as such, the galera begins to look like a collective of bohemians
(Lause 2009; Chauncey 1994).

While the galera's community may be more accurately described, then, as a kind of bohemian cosmopolitanism, queerness can also serve to underscore two unique and seemingly contradictory dimensions of its bohemian cosmopolitan orientation. First, because queerness can also refer to the cultivation of a self and community that are unbound, in flux, and flexible, unrestricted by any notion of a fixed identity (Edelman 1995; Allison 2001), its bohemia is indeed quite queer. Rather than a bohemia that is fixed in a specific area of the city (e.g., Lause 2009; Levin 2010; Wilson 2000; Graña and Graña 1990; Chauncey 1994; Lloyd 2006; Velho 2002), the galera's bohemia is fragmented across space and time—taking place in changing locations and environments and usually at night. As such, "nocturnal bohemia" is the space and time in which the galera's community temporarily manifests as an integrated whole, offering a unique contribution to the growing literature on queer space and time (Halberstam 2005; McCallum and Tuhkanen 2011; Dean 2009; Bersani 1996; Edelman 1998).

The galera's cosmopolitanism is queer along other lines as well. A fair number of scholars have argued that in numerous cultures the notion of a gay identity is seen as Western and, thus, is associated with a "modern" lifestyle (Parker 1999b; Donham 1998; Boellstorff 2005). Seen this way, one might be inclined to think that a bohemian-cosmopolitan community so invested in novel and distant ways of life like the galera would be at the very center of Teresina's LGBT movement. This, however, is far from the case. The galera's nocturnal bohemia and the LGBT movement/gay subculture are quite distinct from one another. Nonnormative expressions of gender/sexuality have always been part of the galera's nocturnal bohemia: women and men donning attire, dancing, and interacting with others in ways not normally considered appropriate for their respective genders. And while it is common knowledge within the galera that a great many participants engage in same-sex sexual practices and relationships, a fair number do not. Unlike many mainstream LGBT events and spaces in Brazil, the galera is generally less divided along lines of gender and sexual object choice and places less emphasis on sex and sexual identity. It is as if the continual growth and visibility of the LGBT community in Teresina has allowed the galera to construct community along lines other than nonnormative gender/sexuality.

The ethos of queerness that structures many of the galera's cosmopolitan desires and practices, then, also shapes the very contours of its bohemia—a fact that seems somewhat appropriate when one considers Teresina's current state of transition—a city thought to be a cultural backwater now experiencing tremendous population growth; a people with greater purchasing power and access to the world than ever before; and an urban landscape dominated by a socially conservative middle class struggling to position itself in a shifting terrain of social distinctions. Thus, queerness as practiced by the galera—fluidity, flexibility, a penchant for the nonnormative, and an openness toward new possibilities—becomes an antidote to such a world in flux, a way of *be-longing in the world at home*. And, as Part II of the book demonstrates, many participants in the galera are successful in their relationships with family members, friends, clients, and employers by relying on such flexibility to creatively maneuver in and out of different subjectivities in a variety of contexts.

FIELDWORK IN A MIDDLE OF NOWHERE

This book is based on 18 months of fieldwork I conducted in Teresina in 2009 and 2010. Prior to that, I also made three separate visits to Teresina to conduct preliminary research during my summers off from graduate school (2006, 2007, and 2008), and before entering graduate school, I spent one full year (2003–2004) teaching English as a second language in Teresina.

Throughout the course of research, I lived in a few different neighborhoods to develop a broad notion of daily life in the city, both within and on the periphery of the East Zone and downtown. Also, by visiting homes of numerous people throughout, I interacted with a wide variety of residents, including middle-class civil servants, doctors, lawyers, academics, business men and women, teachers, small business owners, housewives, and both part-time and full-time domestic servants and their families.

I carried out systematic participant-observation at four primary sites/ events that informants identified as most central to the galera and two additional sites I later identified in 2009. These included: a punk bar/ concert venue, a monthly dance party, a weekly dance party, a warehouse/ performance space, a clothing bazaar, and a bar. Although I engaged a fair number of informants in activity mapping and had several fill out surveys, the majority of my fieldwork consisted of participant-observation and informal interviews. Over 18 months, I accompanied primary participants and a few others throughout their daily lives to learn about how they appropriate outside worlds and how they relate to other Teresinenses (of different social strata, professions, etc.). The kinds of activities I regularly engaged in with participants were: working with coworkers and clients, running errands in all of the city's zones, preparing for events, riding in cars, taking buses, eating at restaurants, cooking, surfing the Internet, socializing with friends, chatting on MSN Instant Messenger, Tweeting on Twitter, watching films, looking for/flirting with potential sex/roman tic partners (an activity common for both men and women), attending religious/spiritual events, going to the theater and the cinema, drinking coffee and beer, and hanging out at the mall. While it is often the case for ethnographers who study sites with which they become quite familiar, it bears noting that partly due to my working in Teresina as an English teacher prior to beginning research, coupled with the extended amount of time I have spent in the city, informants would regularly forget that I was, in fact, conducting research, and not just "hanging out."

In addition to my research on the galera in Teresina, several other experiences in Brazil have informed my research. Over the course of seven years, I spent a total of approximately four months living in São Paulo and two months visiting numerous Brazilian cities and coastal towns (predominantly in the Northeast and Southeast) as well as small countryside towns in Piauí and neighboring states, usually traveling with or staying in the homes of middle-class Brazilians.

NARRATING TERESINA AND THE GALERA

The story I tell of Teresina is at once singular and multiple. It is singular in the sense that I am telling but one of many potential stories to be told about Teresina. My own subjectivity—as a middle-class American male who grew up in a small Midwestern town and has participated in queer artistic circles for the better part of his life—has everything to do with my particular perspective on Brazil, the Northeast, and life in Teresina. This story is equally multiple in the sense that while my focus is predominantly middle-class Teresinenses residing in Teresina, I attempt to offer a variety of stories, renderings, and perspectives of life in such a way that a diverse readership will be able to relate to, at least partially, what it means to be-long in a place like Teresina.

I realize that my discussion of negative characterizations about Teresina, Piauí, runs the risk of offending some. I have chosen not to omit such representations for two important reasons. First, these unfavorable depictions of Teresina, Piauí play a significant role in how many Teresinenses see themselves in relation to their region, nation, and world. Second, while I am aware that restating negative characterizations of a place may indeed have the effect of further concretizing such notions, I hope that by addressing such a discourse head-on, Teresina, Piauí, will provide fodder for critical engagement about hegemonic understandings of place and will stand out as an example of a kind of place that is both far less exceptional and more important than many would like to think.

Throughout the book, I employ different labels and names for the galera in different chapters to illustrate the shifting subject positions that participants take up in different spaces and moments (e.g., "bohemians" in Chap. 4, "black sheep" in Chap. 5, "friends" in Chap. 6). I have changed all of the names of my informants, as well as names of specific events, businesses, and groups, and have divided some informants into multiple personas bearing different names to protect their identities. It is also worth noting that all quotations throughout the book, unless noted, were obtained in Portuguese and later translated into English. Portuguese words are denoted with italics and their translations are delineated by parentheses—for example, "*galera*" ("clique"). Occasionally, though, some words in italics that appear to be English words—for example, *gay* and *shopping*—are, in fact, Portuguese words, pronounced in Portuguese with Brazilian meanings.

REFERENCES

Abbas, Ackbar. 2002. Cosmopolitan De-scriptions: Shanghai and Hong Kong. In *Cosmopolitanism*, ed. Carol A. Breckenridge, Sheldon Pollock, Homi K. Bhabha, and Dipesh Chakrabarty, 209–228. Durham: Duke University Press.
Allison, Anne. 2001. Cyborg Violence: Bursting Borders and Bodies with Queer Machines. *Cultural Anthropology* 16 (2): 237–265.
Amin, Ash, and Stephen Graham. 1997. The Ordinary City. *Transactions of the Institute of British Geographers* 22: 411–429.
Anderson, Benedict. 1983. *Imagined Communities: Reflections on the Origin and Spread of Nationalism*. London/New York: Verso.
Appadurai, Arjun. 1996. *Modernity at Large: Cultural Dimensions of Globalization*. Minneapolis: University of Minnesota Press.
Appadurai, Arjun, and Carol Breckenridge. 1988. Why Public Culture? *Public Culture* 1 (1): 4–9.
Appiah, Kwame Anthony. 1998. Cosmopolitan Patriots. In *Cosmopolitics: Thinking and Feeling Beyond the Nation*, ed. Pheng Cheah and Bruce Robbins, 91–114. Minneapolis: University of Minnesota Press.
Bersani, L. 1996. *Homos*. Cambridge, MA: Harvard University Press.

Besnier, Niko. 2009. *Gossip and the Everyday Production of Politics*. Honolulu: University of Hawai'i Press.

Bettie, Julie. 2003. *Women Without Class: Girls, Race, and Identity*. Berkeley: University of California Press.

Boellstorff, Tom. 2005. *The Gay Archipelago: Sexuality and Nation in Indonesia*. Princeton: Princeton University Press.

Breckenridge, Carol A., Sheldon Pollock, Homi K. Bhabha, and Dipesh Chakrabarty, eds. 2002. *Cosmopolitanism*. Durham: Duke University Press.

Caldeira, Teresa. 2001. *City of Walls: Crime Segregation and Citizenship in São Paulo*. Berkeley: University of California Press.

Calhoun, Craig. 2008. Cosmopolitanism and Nationalism. *Nations and Nationalism* 14 (3): 427–448.

Chan, Brenda. 2006. Virtual Communities and Chinese National Identity. *Journal of Chinese Overseas* 2 (1): 1–32.

Chauncey, George. 1994. *Gay New York: Gender, Urban Culture, and the Making of the Gay Male World, 1890–1940*. New York: Basic Books.

Cheah, Pheng. 1998. The Cosmopolitical—Today. In *Cosmopolitics: Thinking and Feeling Beyond the Nation*, ed. Pheng Cheah and Bruce Robbins, 20–41. Minneapolis: University of Minnesota Press.

Cheah, Pheng, and Bruce Robbins. 1998. *Cosmopolitics: Thinking and Feeling Beyond the Nation*. Minneapolis: University of Minnesota Press.

Clancey, Gregory. 2004. Local Memory and Worldly Narrative: The Remote City in America and Japan. *Urban Studies* 41: 2335–2355.

Condry, Ian. 2001. Japanese Hip-Hop and the Globalization of Popular Culture. In *Urban Life: Readings in the Anthropology of the City*, ed. George Gmelch and Walter Zenner. Prospect Heights: Waveland Press.

Davis, Mike. 2006. *Planet of Slums*. London: Verso.

Dean, Tim. 2009. *Unlimited Intimacy: Reflections on the Subculture of Barebacking*. Chicago: University of Chicago Press.

Dharwadker, Vinay, ed. 2001. *Cosmopolitan Geographies: New Locations in Literature and Culture*. New York: Routledge.

Diouf, Mamadou. 2002. The Senegalese Murid Trade Diaspora and the Making of a Vernacular Cosmopolitanism. In *Cosmopolitanism*, ed. Carol A. Breckenridge, Sheldon Pollock, Homi K. Bhabha, and Dipesh Chakrabarty, 111–137. Durham: Duke University Press.

Donham, Donald. 1998. Freeing South Africa: The "Modernization" of Male-Male Sexuality in Soweto. *Cultural Anthropology* 13 (1): 1–19.

Edelman, Lee. 1995. Queer Theory: Unstating Desire. *GLQ* 2: 343–346.

———. 1998. The Future is Kid Stuff: Queer Theory, Disidentification, and the Death Drive. *Narrative* 6: 18–30.

Fernandes, L. 2006. *India's New Middle Class: Democratic Politics in an Era of Economic Reform*. Minneapolis: University of Minnesota Press.

Fischer, Michael. 2010. The Rhythmic Beat of the Revolution in Iran. *Cultural Anthropology* 25 (3): 497–543.

Friedmann, John. 1986. The World City Hypothesis. *Development and Change* 17: 69–83.

Gontijo, Fabiano. 2009. *O Rei Momo e O Arco-Íris: Homossexualidade e Carnaval no Rio de Janeiro*. Rio de Janeiro: Garamond.

Graña, César, and Marigay Graña. 1990. *On Bohemia: The Code of the Self-Exiled*. New Brunswick: Transaction Publishers.

Green, James. 2000. *Além do Carnaval: A Homossexualidade Masculina no Brasil do Século XX*. São Paulo: Editora da UNESP.

Gregory, Steven. 2007. *The Devil Behind the Mirror: Globalization and Politics in the Dominican Republic*. Berkeley: University of California Press.

Halberstam, Judith. 2005. *In a Queer Time and Place: Transgender Bodies, Subcultural Lives*. New York: New York University Press.

Hall, Stuart. 2003. Political Belonging in a World of Multiple Identities. In *Conceiving Cosmopolitanism: Theory, Context, and Practice*, ed. Steven Vertovec and Robin Cohen, 25–31. Oxford: Oxford University Press.

Hannerz, Ulf. 1990. Cosmopolitans and Locals in World Culture. In *Global Culture*, ed. Mike Featherstone, 237–252. London: Sage.

Heiman, Rachel, Carla Freeman, and Mark Liechty eds. 2012. *The Global Middle Classes: Theorizing Through Ethnography*. Santa Fe: School for Advanced Research Press.

Holston, James. 1989. *The Modernist City: An Anthropological Critique of Brasília*. Chicago: University of Chicago Press.

IBGE. 2017. Teresina. *Censo.* https://cidades.ibge.gov.br/brasil/pi/teresina/panorama. Accessed 1 Feb 2018.

Jefferson, Mark. 1939. The Law of the Primate City. *Geographical Review* 29: 226–232.

Koonings, Kees, and Dirk Krujit. 2007. *Fractured Cities: Social Exclusion, Urban Violence and Contested Spaces in Latin America*. London: Zed Books.

Kulick, Don. 1998. *Travesti: Sex, Gender, and Culture among Brazilian Transgendered Prostitutes*. Chicago: University of Chicago Press.

Lamonte, Michelle. 1992. *Money, Morals, and Manners: The Culture of the French and the American Upper-Middle Class*. Chicago: University of Chicago Press.

Lause, Mark A. 2009. *The Antebellum Crisis & America's First Bohemians*. Kent: Kent State University Press.

Levin, Joanna. 2010. *Bohemia in America, 1858–1920*. Stanford: Stanford University Press.

Liechty, Mark. 2003. *Suitably Modern: Making Middle-Class Culture in a New Consumer Society*. Princeton: Princeton University Press.

Lima, Gerson Portela. 2003. *Atlas da exclusão no Piauí*. Teresina: Fundação CEPRO.

Linklater, Andrew. 1999. Cosmopolitan Citizenship. In *Kimberly Hutchings and Roland Dannreuther*, ed. Cosmopolitan Citizenship, 35–59. London: Macmillan Press.

Lloyd, Richard. 2006. *Neo-Bohemia: Art and Commerce in the Postindustrial City*. New York: Routledge.

Malcomson, Scott L. 1998. The Varieties of Cosmopolitan Experience. In *Cosmopolitics: Thinking and Feeling Beyond the Nation*, ed. Pheng Cheah and Bruce Robbins, 233–245. Minneapolis: University of Minnesota Press.

Manalansan, Martin F.I.V. 2003. *Global Divas: Filipino Gay Men in the Diaspora*. Durham: Duke University Press.

McCallum, Cecilia. 2005. Racialized Bodies, Naturalized Classes: Moving through the City of Salvador da Bahia. *American Ethnologist* 32 (1): 100–117.

McCallum, E.L., and Mikko Tuhkanen. 2011. *Queer Times, Queer Becomings*. Albany: SUNY Press.

Montgomery, Mark R. 2008. The Urban Transformation of the Developing World. *Science* 319: 761–764.

Nascimento, Francisco Alcides do. 2007. Cajuína e cristalina: as transformações espaciais vistas pelos cronistas que atuaram nos jornais de Teresina entre 1950 e 1970. *Revista Brasileira de História* 27 (53): 195–214.

Novak, David. 2010. Cosmopolitanism, Remediation, and the Ghost World of Bollywood. *Cultural Anthropology* 25 (1): 40–72.

O'Dougherty, Maureen. 2002. *Consumption Intensified: The Politics of Middle-Class Daily Life in Brazil*. Durham: Duke University Press.

Ong, Aihwa. 1998. Flexible Citizenship among Chinese Cosmopolitans. In *Cosmopolitics: Thinking and Feeling Beyond the Nation*, ed. Pheng Cheah and Bruce Robbins, 134–162. Minneapolis: University of Minnesota Press.

Parker, Richard. 1999a. *Beneath the Equator: Cultures of Desire, Male Homosexuality, and Emerging Gay Communities in Brazil*. London: Routledge.

———. 1999b. 'Within Four Walls': Brazilian Sexual Culture and HIV/AIDS. In *Culture, Society and Sexuality: A Reader*, ed. Richard Parker and Peter Aggleton. London: UCL Press.

Pollock, Sheldon. 2002. Cosmopolitan and Vernacular in History. In *Cosmopolitanism*, ed. Carol A. Breckenridge, Sheldon Pollock, Homi K. Bhabha, and Dipesh Chakrabarty, 15–53. Durham: Duke University Press.

Potuoğlu-Cook, Öykü. 2006. Beyond the Glitter: Belly Dance and Neoliberal Gentrification in Istanbul. *Cultural Anthropology* 21 (4): 633–660.

Rapport, Nigel, and Ronald Stade. 2007. A Cosmopolitan Turn—Or Return? *Social Anthropology* 15 (2): 223–235.

Rée, Jonathan. 1998. Cosmopolitanism and the Experience of Nationality. In *Cosmopolitics: Thinking and Feeling Beyond the Nation*, ed. Pheng Cheah and Bruce Robbins, 77–90. Minneapolis: University of Minnesota Press.

Robbins, Bruce. 1998. Comparative Cosmopolitanisms. In *Cosmopolitics: Thinking and Feeling Beyond the Nation*, ed. Pheng Cheah and Bruce Robbins, 246–264. Minneapolis: University of Minnesota Press.

Robinson, Jennifer. 2006. *Ordinary Cities: Between Modernity and Development*. London/New York: Routledge.

Sassen, Saskia. 1991. *The Global City: New York, London, Tokyo*. Princeton: Princeton University Press.

Schein, Louisa. 1998. Importing Miao Brethren to Hmong America: A Not-So-Stateless Transnationalism. In *Cosmopolitics: Thinking and Feeling Beyond the Nation*, ed. Pheng Cheah and Bruce Robbins, 163–191. Minneapolis: University of Minnesota Press.

Scheld, Suzanne. 2007. Youth Cosmopolitanism: Clothing, the City and Globalization in Dakar, Senegal. *City and Society* 19 (2): 232–253.

Scheper-Hughes, Nancy. 1992. *Death Without Weeping: The Violence of Everyday Life in Brazil*. Berkeley: University of California Press.

Simone, Abdu Malik. 2004. *For the city yet to come: Changing African Life in Four Cities*. Durham: Duke University Press.

Velho, Gilberto. 2002. *A Utopia Urbana: Um Estudo de Antropologia Social*. Rio de Janeiro: Jorge Zahar Editor.

Weiss, Brad. 2002. Thug Realism: Inhabiting Fantasy in Urban Tanzania. *Cultural Anthropology* 17 (1): 93–124.

Wilson, Elizabeth. 2000. *Bohemians: The Glamorous Outcasts*. New Brunswick: Rutgers University Press.

Wilson, Ara. 2004. *The Intimate Economies of Bangkok: Tomboys, Tycoons, and Avon Ladies in the Global City*. Berkeley: University of California Press.

Wood, Allen W. 1998. Kant's Project for Perpetual Peace. In *Cosmopolitics: Thinking and Feeling Beyond the Nation*, ed. Pheng Cheah and Bruce Robbins, 59–76. Minneapolis: University of Minnesota Press.

Zhang, Li. 2006. Contesting Spatial Modernity in Late Socialist China. *Current Anthropology* 47 (3): 461–484.

CHAPTER 2

From Terehell to Terenowhere

Abstract The chapter begins by investigating Teresina's inescapable heat to show how the experience of extreme heat combined with an imagined superior and "cooler" outside world manifests as *be-longing*—a desire for Teresina, Piauí, to be seen as a place worthy of recognition. The chapter introduces the reader to the region's long history of drought, poverty, and marginal position in the national imaginary and examines how residents perceive and deal with the heat on a daily basis, revealing how this experience contributes to their sense of be-longing in the city. The chapter sets the reader up for the subsequent chapter's discussion of Teresina's present moment—a city undergoing acute urbanization and socioeconomic change, and, therefore, a chance for residents to finally claim a rightful place for themselves.

Keywords Belonging • Heat • Marginalization • Northeastern Brazil

When preparing to head outside into the hell of the day, motorcycle taxi drivers in Teresina grab their jean jackets to protect their arms from the sun, maids lather their faces and arms in sunscreen, and those with cars hop into them and crank up the air-conditioning immediately. On the street, pedestrians and bus riders are particularly adept at seeking shade, even if that means huddling up close to strangers. Especially between the hours of 9 am and 5 pm, at each turn of a corner pedestrians automatically

T. E. Murphy, *Queerly Cosmopolitan*,
https://doi.org/10.1007/978-3-030-00296-1_2

walk toward the side of the street where a wall or tree casts a shadow. Because shade is not always present, pedestrians often create their own shade by using parasols, felt cowboy hats, straw hats, t-shirts, plastic folders, backpacks, and hands to protect their faces from the sun's stinging and staining rays. As the sun changes position throughout the day, bus stops take on lives of their own, morphing organically as people waiting rearrange themselves within slowly moving shadows cast by lamp posts, street venders' umbrellas, and the fat oval leaves of the almendoeira trees. On buses, the shaded side of the vehicle quickly becomes packed as riders avoid sitting on the hot sunbaked plastic seats. Bus riders keep their hair tied back, fan themselves with notebooks, peel their shirts loose from their sticky torsos, and wipe the sweat from their brows. After lunch, manual laborers nap shirtless on their backs in any shade they can find, while state bureaucrats wake themselves with refreshing cool showers and hop back into their air-conditioned cars to return to work. Downtown, venders sell ice-cold coconut water at most every intersection, and unofficial security guards hold vigil over parked cars and shade them, placing broken-down cardboard boxes on their windshields in exchange for spare change. Residents of all walks of life find relief in consuming ice cream made with regional fruits, drinking cold juice made of cashew apples, and sipping on the "coldest beer in Brazil." Upon arriving at a private residence or an office, the host or secretary offers a small cup of cold water to guests; if not, the guests will ask for one. In the homes of relatives and close friends, men are invited to remove their shirts and guests know they are always welcome to take a shower or a dip in the pool to cool off.

Raquel's girlfriend, Nenê, lives downtown—Teresina's hottest sector. Over the years, downtown has gotten even hotter as pavement and concrete buildings and walls replace shady mango trees and wild grassy areas. Despite Nenê's meager salary and financial obligations to her household, she has finally saved up enough to have a plaster ceiling and air conditioner installed in her bedroom (the majority of homes in Teresina have vaulted roofs made of wooden beams and ceramic tiles with no internal ceilings). One evening, visiting Nenê at her modest home, it became clear to me just how difficult living in such a hot place can be for some.

If it were not for the acrid waft of burning trash floating over the wall and through the bars of Nenê's living room window, I would swear that the outside air was completely still. It's almost midnight. As I wait for Raquel to pick me up, I am startled by a series of loud metal banging sounds behind me that quickly turn into a high pitched *click-click-click-click-click-click-click* and then only a soft hum. Nenê has just plugged in the old black metal fan mounted on the plastic patio chair beside her. She is sitting at her desk surfing the Internet on her yellowed desktop computer, searching for synopses of recent films in Spanish for her students' presentations this week. As she leans into her monitor to read the synopses, she fans her bosom and wipes her sweat-beaded brow. Nenê has just returned to her desk after having taken yet another shower to cool off. As is typical for this time of year, the water wasn't even tepid. It was the usual inescapable warm, thanks to the day's unrelenting heat. Her hair is wet, tied up in a bun on the top of her head. In a little while, she will engage in a practice that she's enacted ever since she was a little girl. Readying herself for bed, Nenê will fill up a plastic bucket of water, attach her hammock to the hooks bolted into her walls and then, dipping her fingers into the water, she'll begin to flick drops of water all over the cotton weave. Before crawling in, she'll reposition the chair with the fan so it will blow directly on her, strip down to her undergarments, and slide in. Multiple times throughout the night, Nenê will wake up sweating in her dry hammock and repeat the process. When I ask Nenê to describe how she feels about the city's heat, she tells me:

> It's the only thing that really bothers me about this city. You know how I love Teresina and its people, but the heat...I can't stand it one bit. It's no joke. During B-R-O BRÓ it's even worse. I get a headache that lasts four months. I swear. For we Teresinenses, it's our most difficult and desperate moment. Each year I get to thinking that I really hope we are able to make it through this B-R-O BRÓ.

Nenê, like most all Teresinenses, refers to this particularly hot season as *"B-R-O-BRO."* It is known as the hottest, driest, and sunniest season of the year in Teresina, and it is named as such because it includes all of the months that end in *"BRO"*—*setembro, outubro, novembro,* and *dezembro.* During this season, the daily temperature averages a high of 97°F (36°C), whereas the daily average highs for Fortaleza (the capital of the neighboring state, Ceará) and Rio de Janeiro at this same time of year are around 87°F (30°C) and 83°F (28°C), respectively (WeatherSpark 2018). Rain is considered something of a godsend at this time of year. While children run outside to "bathe in the rain," friends in various locations across the city tweet about the refreshing rainfall on the place they often call "Terehell."

While it is always hot in Teresina, these four months are particularly scorching, and even though this season is by far the most consistently hot, it does not have to be B-R-O BRÓ for people to be bothered by the climate. Teresinenses regularly voice their frustrations to friends, family, and strangers about the unbearably hot days and weeks that pepper the entire year in Teresina. They complain, "*Eita, que calor!*" (Damn, what heat!), "*Tá quente pra porra!*" (It's so fucking hot!), "*Que calor infernal, minha gente*" (What hellish heat, you guys), "*Essa cidade tá infernalizando a gente*" (This city is putting us through hell), "*Não aguento mais desse calor. Deus me livre*" (I can't stand this heat. God help me). And they also joke, "*É tão quente que a gente tem que passar protector solar inclusive na noite!*" (It's so hot that we have to put sunscreen on even at night!), and sometimes quip when people ask why it's so hot, "*É porque o diabo mora aqui!*" (It's because the devil lives here!). Even those with air conditioners cannot completely escape the heat, as movement in the city, at best, requires traversing from one air-conditioned space to another, and even that kind of lifestyle is a rarity in Teresina, where almost no homes, schools, or office buildings are entirely air-conditioned. To a certain degree, then, to live in Teresina is to weather the heat as well as all it symbolizes. And it is heat's prevalence, both discursive and experiential, that contributes to many Teresinenses' conviction that their city is one of the hottest places on earth.

The sheer impossibility of ignoring Teresina's heat—whether due to the way it feels, its prevalence in daily discourse, or its various influences on the general public—has encouraged me to treat it as a principal character in this story about Teresina. Anthropologist Michael Taussig points out that heat, somewhat unexpectedly, rarely takes center stage in writing and film and is more commonly used either as a "prop" or as a "device to propel a plot" (2004: 32). Using Branislaw Malinowski's *Argonauts of the Western Pacific* (1922) and Bradd Shore's *Sala'ilua: A Samoan Mystery* (1982) as examples, Taussig asserts that ethnographers tend to either use it as a launch pad to embark on a discussion of something entirely different or omit it from their publications altogether (2004: 33). Even in Claude Levi-Strauss' famous *Tristes Tropiques* (1961), heat is surprisingly given very little attention. Here, heat merely serves Levi-Strauss to indicate his being near the tropics (1961: 95) or to briefly add to his description of the context in which he is writing (1961: 305; 353; 409). Similarly, in film and fiction, Taussig argues, heat becomes overshadowed by something else (2004: 36). Despite the growing literature on climate anthropology (e.g., Crate 2011; Crate and Nuttall 2009; Strauss and Orlove 2003; Peterson and Broad 2009), Erik Klinenberg's seminal study of the tragic 1995 Chicago heat wave (2002) still stands out as one of the few exceptions to Taussig's claim.

Heat means something special in Teresina because heat in the Brazilian Northeast symbolizes backwardness, poverty, the raw, and the exposed. In a region notorious for its long history of excessively high temperatures, devastating droughts, and extreme poverty, heat is often conceived of as threatening to the stability of life. What does it mean, then, to be from a place so hot that it merits the nickname, "Terehell?" And how does such a name relate to how people view their city and themselves?

What follows is an investigation into these questions, first through an explanation of the pervasive middle-class discourse of *fora*,[1] and, second, through a brief discussion of the cultural and historical context of the region. In doing so, I will attempt to show how the experience of extreme and inescapable heat in "Terehell," combined with an imagined superior and cooler outside world—fora—manifests as *be*-longing: a desire for Teresina to be seen as a place worthy of recognition.

For Teresina's growing middle class especially, exposure to more media and increased opportunities for travel has encouraged residents to begin to understand themselves less in terms of the countryside hometowns from which they hail or their immediate neighbors in Teresina, and more in terms of their entire city, region, nation, and world. As Teresinenses make new forays into these wider spheres, their city's caustic sun and heat follow them via the notion of *fora*, contributing to residents' sense of placeness and be-longing in the world. The term "*fora*" means "outside" in Brazilian Portuguese, and as in English, it is used throughout Brazil to refer to the opposite of "inside." In everyday conversation, fora can also be used to index places lying beyond Brazil's borders, connoting a somewhere usually imagined to be culturally and economically superior, more developed, more progressive, and whiter. Thus, in much of Brazil, the

---

[1] "*Fora*" (outside) is a term that is often used to signal a particular set of foreign places and cultures imagined to be superior.

phrase *"quero morar fora"* means "I want to live abroad." Yet what is peculiar about fora is that it also connotes cool temperatures, rendering the experience of cool weather as something to be desired. In São Paulo, friends of mine like to joke about how fashionistas will take the very first instance of slightly chilly weather to wrap up in a fancy scarf or to show off their newest pair of stylish boots. It is almost expected that Brazilians who travel abroad to somewhere snowy post photos of themselves happily bundled up on social media sites like Orkut or Facebook. Even in the state of Piauí, of which Teresina is the capital, a jazz festival that takes place on a higher elevation than Teresina where temperatures can drop to as low as 65°F has prompted a number of attendees unaccustomed to the chilly weather to wear ski jackets, drink warm beverages, and even refer to the small town as "the Switzerland of Piauí."

When positioned next to the pervasive middle-class discourse of an imagined wealthier and more sophisticated fora, then, Teresina feels especially hellish—and not just to the touch, but also in terms of what this hot weather can symbolize: poverty, backwardness, and a general lack of importance. Such a perspective was not born overnight. In part, it stems from living in a region that has been marginalized for a good part of Brazilian history.

FAR FROM FORA: THE BRAZILIAN NORTHEAST

The Brazilian Northeast is vast, occupying roughly 20% of Brazil's territory. Its population alone exceeds 45 million, roughly one-third of the nation's total population. If the Northeast were its own country, it would be ranked the third largest in Latin America. Although the region's major coastal cities—Salvador, Recife, and Fortaleza—are densely populated and rapidly growing, the majority of *Nordestinos* (Northeasterners) reside in the rural heart of the region, comprising 46% of Brazil's total rural population. Popularly referred to as the Sertão, this inland portion of the Northeast encompasses rural areas of nine states that are subjected to unwavering high temperatures and long periods of drought, sometimes lasting from one to three years. Extreme poverty pervades both rural and urban settings, and combined, the Northeast accounts for about one half of the nation's poor (Araújo 2004), making the region's extreme heat almost synonymous with its extreme poverty. Although new industries in the region are on the rise, agriculture remains the dominant sector of the economy and produces far less than the affluent Southeast.

Explanations for Brazil's regional disparity point to a long history of social inequality and economic changes that occurred both on regional and national scales. In the 1950s, economist Celso Furtado argued that Brazil's regionally centered agro-export economic base, in which natural resources were extracted, sent through production, and finally exported abroad, was destined for a crisis of uneven development (Furtado 1965). Once the Portuguese lost their near-monopoly of the sugar market to the Dutch in the mid-seventeenth century, sugar plantations in the Northeast lost their economic promise for the colony. In the early eighteenth century, the mining boom shifted the colony's economic stronghold to the Center-South, which was replaced by the coffee boom in the Southeast during the nineteenth century. These events left the Northeast to sustain itself in the form of a subsistence economy, ultimately limiting its capacity for economic growth. Wealthy landowners—first, feudal barons and later, large landowners—expanded westward, extending farmlands and slaves/workers into the hinterlands to sustain the regional economy as the population grew (Furtado 1965). It was this westward expansion that paved the way for the establishment of Oeiras in 1759, Piauí's first capital. Less than one century later, the capital was moved North to Teresina in the hopes that its intersecting rivers Poti and Parnaíba would make it an important inland hub of commerce and political power for the region (Fundação CEPRO 2002: 12).

Brazil's export-based economy proved problematic not only by creating disparities of wealth among regions; each industrial boom was followed by a crisis that resulted in economic recession and decades of stagnation for the country at large. After the coffee crisis of the 1930s, policy makers offered a solution: import substitution. By restricting imported goods and replacing them with internally produced ones, industry in the South would be able to sustain its growth. For the Northeast, however, the solution backfired. With a national ban on imports, the Northeast was forced to purchase goods from the South at even higher prices, thereby further weakening its economy. Although import substitution sustained the national economy, it only exacerbated regional economic disparity (Furtado 1965).

An equally salient force contributing to poverty within the region has been a persistent economic disparity between the elite and "popular" classes due to widespread landlessness in the countryside and neo-feudalism. In 1960, two-thirds of the 25 million people living in the Northeast were living in what Furtado called a "pre-political state" (Furtado 1965: 128). In other words, many rural Nordestinos were dispersed across immense estates, fighting for survival in often the least fertile and most drought-susceptible areas. In relative isolation, they relied on the paternalistic protection of landowners while living and growing crops close in proximity only to family members and the occasional neighbor. For many rural Nordestinos, the notion of instituting social change collectively or by calling attention to a public authority was almost inconceivable (Lambert 1959).

Today in the Northeast, many of the conditions established during the colonial period remain. In rural areas, inequality persists as many small farmers, sharecroppers, and renters still lack resources for survival, much less opportunities for a better life, and rarely does one hear of successful attempts to redistribute wealth and power in the region. Even in years when there is a normal amount of rainfall, these farmers have difficulty accumulating a surplus, a necessity for when drought occurs (Araújo 2004: 23). During such times, desperate families commonly relinquish their plots of land to large landowners at extremely low prices and migrate to the cities (Araújo 2004: 23), and, as a result, rural-urban migration and urban poverty are on the rise. While in Teresina, I often heard friends voice frustration about families they knew personally who were involved in corruption scandals and other more direct forms of exploiting the rural poor; the stories ranged from a politician who built a façade of a school for a photo shoot instead of a functioning one in order to profit from the project, to politicians whose children have money in bank accounts under the names of their close friends, to people with indentured servants.

Throughout the region, capital cities are the most promising alternatives for the rural poor, and except for Piauí, all the capitals are situated along the Atlantic coast, attracting tourism and investment from inside and outside Brazil. Though Brazilians from other regions visit cities and vacation in resorts scattered along the Northeast's beach-lined coast, its reputation as the country's hottest and poorest region renders it marginal in the Brazilian imaginary (Fig. 2.1).

Fig. 2.1 Map of Brazil by Krista Chael, 2018

THE TWO BRAZILS

Since at least the turn of the twentieth century, the Northeast and its residents have been understood as the "Other Brazil" and the Brazilian Other, respectively—a discourse that has been concretized through the recycling of tropes about the region and its inhabitants in social studies and stories. Despite the colorful distinctions that Nordestinos make, comparing one

Northeastern state and its people to another—emphasizing differences in accent/dialect, appearance, work ethic, intelligence, food, and the like— depictions in writing, film, and television tend to lump all nine states into one homogeneous region and people.

Os Sertões (Rebellion in the Backlands), by Euclides da Cunha, was originally published in 1902 and is perhaps the most famous portrait of the Northeast to date. A story of war at the end of the nineteenth century between the Brazilian army and the Nordestino religious leader Antonio Conselheiro and his followers, the account is as much an attempt at salvage ethnography as it is a battle narrative. Da Cunha documents the rough ecology and human existence of the Northeast before its "backward races" become extinct (da Cunha 1944: xxxi). Rife with a mixture of poetics and scientific language, da Cunha's portrayal of the "agonized," "parched," and "tortured" flora of the extremely hot and dry Sertão leaves the reader with an impression that the only motivation to continue living in the region is to avoid death, a theme that carries over into his representation of the people (da Cunha 1944: 30–31). Da Cunha repeatedly asserts throughout his account that a rural Northeastern "race" or "stock" is the result of a people who have spent no less than three centuries of isolation at war with their physical environment, culminating into a distinct phenotype and way of life.

More than half a century after Os Sertões was published, depictions of the Northeast and Nordestinos continued to portray the region in a similar light, complicated now by narratives casting Nordestinos as class victims. First published in 1959, French sociologist Jacques Lambert wrote Os Dois Brasis, (The Two Brazils), a critical investigation of the Brazilian socioeconomic structure, arguing that, under one nation, economic disparity makes for the coexistence of two distinct countries divided by time. Lambert elucidates:

> Between the old Brazil and the new there are centuries of distance; throughout the years the difference of the rhythms of evolution have resulted in the formation of two societies, different because they are not contemporaries. [...] There are two countries, between which it is difficult to distinguish the true one. (1959: 109)[2]

---

[2] The translation from Portuguese is my own. The original reads, "Entre o velho Brasil e o novo existem séculos de distância; no correr dos anos a diferença dos ritmos de evolução ocasionou

For Lambert, then, the two Brazils are divided primarily between the underdeveloped Northeast and the rapidly developing Southeast and South. Lambert's treatise aimed to expose inequality in the country through a geographical and historical lens, but by asserting that the Northeast is not only poor but also trapped in the past he further reinforces the notion that the "Nordestino" is essentially different from the "Brazilian." Similar depictions also surface in Brazilian cinema. In 1963, a film based on Graciliano Ramos' 1938 novel, *"Vidas Secas"* ("Dry Lives"), exposed the desperate situation of a Nordestino family wandering the sweltering Sertão in the hopeless search of a better life, a theme that would be reappropriated in numerous other portraits of Nordestinos, including *"Bye Bye Brasil,"* directed by Carlos Diegues (1979), and *"O Caminho nas Nuvens"* ("The Middle of the World"), directed by Vicente Amorim (2003), in which the struggle to escape poverty is only slightly or never resolved. In many of these works, the same imagery that da Cunha put forth so long ago appears yet again—destitution, a lack of education, a devoutly Catholic and superstitious religiosity, determination, and isolation in the blistering, godforsaken Sertão.

IMAGINING TERESINA, PIAUÍ

Most Brazilians have very little idea of what Teresina, Piauí, actually looks like. The Northeast gets most of its exposure through tourism. Along the coast, small beach towns and larger cities cater to tourists from all over Brazil and abroad. But Teresina's inland location, Piauí's comparatively small coast, and the distance from major tourist attractions in the region makes for limited tourism and national exposure. Before former president "Lula" was elected in 2002, images of the state of Piauí had seldom appeared in the national media. Yet when Lula spearheaded his antihunger campaign, he focused on two of the poorest municipalities in Brazil—Acauã and Guaribas—both of which are located in the South of Piauí. Though ostensibly well intentioned, this exposure reinforced negative stereotypes about the Northeast and Teresina, Piauí in particular. Thus, with images of Acauã and Guaribas flooding national television,

a formação de duas sociedades, diferentes porque não são contemporáneas. [...] Existem dois países entre os quais é difícil distinguir o verdadeiro" (109).

any assumption that the next-to-invisible Teresina, Piauí, epitomizes Northeastern destitution, lack of education, extreme heat, suffering, and isolation was confirmed.

In 2003, when I first began teaching English at a language school in Teresina, I was surprised to hear my students—mostly teenagers from upwardly mobile and influential families—tell me stories about their city and state's inferior image in the national imaginary. Since then, I have heard a select few of these stories repeated on numerous occasions from middle-class residents of various ages. One is that the famous Brazilian late-night television show host Joe Soares once said on national television that their state is "*o cu do mundo*" (literally meaning "the asshole of the world" but probably closer to the US colloquialism "the armpit of America"). Another story refers to the president of the Brazilian branch of Phillips Electronics who was quoted as saying that no one would mind if the state of Piauí were to cease to exist. And yet another tells of how the Brazilian government once published a textbook for public schools and failed to include the state of Piauí on the national map.

Less notorious but equally significant are a few additional stories that I heard from participants in the galera.[3] When I asked my friend Lydia about the matter, she explained that she cannot understand why people bother dwelling on such thoughts, especially considering all the richness that Teresina and Piauí have to offer—from beautiful landscapes to peoples' intimate relationships with flora, fauna, and the land. Nevertheless, she followed up her comment by telling me a couple more stories of Piauí's unimportance. She remarked that the creator of the new Rio de Janeiro-based magazine *Revista Piauí*, whose target audience is highbrow left-leaning Brazilian intellectuals, chose the name "Piauí" because of his fascination with words containing numerous vowels. "He said it sounded 'exotic,' denying any reference to the state of Piauí," she added. To add insult to injury, a contributing author to the same magazine later published a travel piece about his lengthy excursion along the Northeastern coast, describing each of the states' beaches, except those of Piauí. Lydia said that after receiving criticism from *Piauienses*

---

[3] The "galera" refers to the clique of people who come together to form Teresina's nocturnal bohemia (Chap. 4).

(residents of Piauí) for his omission, he defended it by saying that the article had a short word limit, and, besides, Piauí's coast is the smallest and least significant in the region (Fig. 2.2).

In my own travels throughout Brazil, I, too, have listened to similar negative characterizations of the city and state. While staying at the home of a friend in Recife, a Northeastern coastal city with nearly twice the population of Teresina, a fellow Northeasterner now living in Brasília tried to correct me when I told him I was doing anthropological research in Teresina. "You don't mean Teresina. You mean in the South of Piauí at the famous archeological site, Serra da Capivara, right?" When I corrected him, explaining that I am a cultural anthropologist and was conducting fieldwork in Teresina proper, he looked at me confused and exclaimed, "But why? There's nothing there but heat! You should study Salvador or Rio." When I retorted that those cities are overrun with foreign researchers and that a study of Teresina has the potential to offer a different under-standing of urban life in Brazil, he raised his eyebrows, chuckled, and shook his head saying, "Well, for me, it sucks." One time in São Paulo, I accompanied a Teresinense friend of mine to a poetry reading at the home of one of his classmates. At one point in the evening, my friend casually disclosed that he is from Teresina. The host blurted out, "Wow!" and proceeded to announce, "Hey everybody, did you know that Romero is from Piauí? I never would have guessed it!" Another classmate chimed in, "I know. I recently met a woman from Recife. I couldn't believe it. She was so erudite!"

According to these characterizations, the city of Teresina is hot as hell with nothing to offer and its residents are all uneducated, while the state of Piauí is essentially the armpit of Brazil, worthless to the nation and the tourist, and reducible to an "exotic" sounding word bereft of any mean-ing. Since my initial visit to Teresina in 2003, I have been baffled time and time again that such a place—or any place for that matter—could continu-ally receive such negative attention. My suspicion, however, is that Teresina, Piauí, is not so unique in its perceived "unimportance," and I am inclined to take seriously Gregory Clancey's claim that "the 'out-of-the-way' may indeed be an urban legend unconsciously sustained by our focus on a hierarchical urban network of globe-spanning proportions" (2004: 2335). In other words, Teresina, Piauí's perceived lack of importance is more the rule than the exception to the rule when considering "impor-tant" cities worldwide.

Fig. 2.2   The tenth issue of *Revista Piauí* for sale at a newsstand in downtown Teresina

CONCLUSION

This glimpse into the historical and political-economic context of Teresina combined with the daily experience of extreme heat and a prevalent discourse of a far-away *fora* conveys just how easy it might be to think of Teresina as a middle-of-nowhere hell. Being an outsider (and from *fora*, no less), I was especially prone to hear about such depictions of Teresina, Piauí. That said, as Teresinenses go about their daily lives, it is only in specific instances that they are confronted with such notions—instances that reflect their complex relationship to them. On the one hand, reifying the notion that *fora* is quite far from Teresina can exacerbate many residents' dissatisfaction with their city and its marginality. On the other hand, numerous Teresinenses rely on such stereotypical portraits of Teresina, Piauí, and the Northeast as excessively hot, poor, isolated, and backward in moments when they wish to demonstrate their own proximity to *fora*, contrasting their daily practices and experiences from such "unsophisticated" ways of life. I will conclude here with a story that illustrates the latter.

One bright, steamy morning during my first few weeks of teaching at the foreign language school, I accidentally took the wrong—and falsely advertised, "air-conditioned"—bus from my new neighborhood to work. Within a matter of minutes, I found myself crossing over a river and heading down a major boulevard into an even hotter, more densely populated, and lively commercial area that looked like a downtown. Unlike the sparse, suburban, and increasingly commercial East Zone that my bosses referred to as "Teresina" on our chilly car ride from the airport to my new apartment, this urban area was packed with pedestrians, bicycles, motorcyclists, street vendors, and bustling plazas. Vibrant colors and sounds accompanied the bricolage of buildings, bodies, and bounty before me: students in school uniforms joking with one another beneath the shade of a tree, an elderly woman on a park bench wiping the sweat from her forehead, two young women walking with a parasol, middle-aged men on a corner chatting with their hot bellies exposed, and street vendors beneath giant umbrellas selling everything from raw cashews to flip-flops to produce to fresh coconut water. After managing to locate the correct bus and arriving to work nearly an hour late, I walked into the cold sterile lobby of the school drenched in sweat. I explained to my bosses and the staff why I was late but could not mask the excitement I felt from discovering this part of town. They laughed, and one of my bosses joked that only a crazy gringo would be impressed with downtown Teresina. She commented, "Seriously, it's hot as hell and crowded with people, and there's nowhere to park! I do everything to avoid going there."

Over time, I discovered that most everyone I encountered was much more familiar with downtown than I was initially led to believe. It is not that Teresina's downtown is unimportant to the city—after all, it is home to city hall, the courthouse, the city's biggest hospitals and clinics, elite private schools, and a number of buildings and offices for employees of the state. But compared to the newer suburban East Zone of the city where the foreign language school is located, downtown represents for many upwardly mobile residents exactly what they are trying to escape—heat, poverty, and a "Third-World"-looking urban landscape.

REFERENCES

Bye Bye Brasil. 1979. Film. Brazil: Carlos Diegues.

Clancey, Gregory. 2004. Local Memory and Worldly Narrative: The Remote City in America and Japan. *Urban Studies* 41: 2335–2355.

Crate, Susan A. 2011. Climate and Culture: Anthropology in the Era of Contemporary Climate Change. *Annual Review of Anthropology* 40: 175–194.

Crate, Susan A., and Mark Nuttall, eds. 2009. *Anthropology and Climate Change: From Encounters to Actions*. Walnut Creek: Left Coast Press.

Cunha, Euclides da. 1944. *Rebellions in the Backlands*. Translation by Samuel Putnam *Os Sertões* [1902]. Chicago: University of Chicago Press.

de Araújo, Tânia Bacelar, and Paulo Simões. 2004. Northeast, Northeasts: What Northeast? *Latin American Perspectives* 31 (2): 16–41.

Fundação CEPRO. 2002. *Piauí: Visão Global*. Teresina: Fundação CEPRO.

Furtado, Celso. 1965. *Diagnosis of the Brazilian Crisis*. Berkeley: University of California Press.

Klinenberg, Eric. 2002. *Heat Wave: A Social Autopsy of Disaster in Chicago*. Chicago: University of Chicago Press.

Lambert, Jacques. 1959. *Os Dois Brasis*. Rio de Janeiro: Centro Brasileiro de Pesquisas Educacionais.

Levi-Strauss, Claude. 1961. *Tristes Tropiques*, Trans. John Russell. New York: Criterion Books.

Malinowski, Branislaw. 1922. *Argonauts of the Western Pacific*. London: Routledge.

O Caminho nas Nuvens. 2003. Film. Brazil: Vicente Amorim.

Peterson, Nicole, and Kenneth Broad. 2009. Climate and Weather Discourse in Anthropology: From Determinism to Uncertain Futures. In *Anthropology and Climate Change: From Encounters to Actions*, ed. Susan A. Crate and Mark Nuttall, 70–86. Walnut Creek: Left Coast Press.

Ramos, Graciliano. 1938. *Vidas Secas*. Rio de Janeiro: Livraria José Olympio Editora.

Shore, Bradd. 1982. *Sala'ilua: A Samoan Mystery*. New York: Columbia University Press.

Strauss, Sarah, and Benjamin S. Orlove, eds. 2003. *Weather, Climate, Culture*. New York: Berg.

Taussig, Michael T. 2004. *My Cocaine Museum*. Chicago: University of Chicago Press.

Vidas Secas. 1967. Film. Brazil: Nelson Pereira dos Santos.

WeatherSpark. 2018. Average Weather in Teresina. https://weatherspark. com/y/30735/Average-Weather-in-Teresina-Brazil-Year-Round. Accessed 23 Jan 2018.

CHAPTER 3

Chique Distinction in a Big Small Town

Abstract The chapter begins with a portrait of Teresina's dominant sectors, revealing how practices of social distinction are embedded in the urban landscape. The chapter then investigates more closely how residents' public demonstrations of sophistication interact with the built environment in the construction of an array of sophisticated people and places throughout the city. In the context of a rapidly growing provincial city where aspirations and anxiety around belonging are especially pronounced, to be invested in demonstrations of sophistication is to long for inclusion in the upwardly mobile echelons of Teresina's society. The chapter argues that establishing a sense of belonging among Teresina's upwardly mobile residents is not reducible to middle-class membership; it can only be grasped through the nuance of local understandings of social distinction.

Keywords Middle class • Uncertainty • Distinction • Upward mobility

If you happen to be awake around the balmy hour of six in the morning, just after the mango-colored sun peeks up over the crowns of the babaçu and carnauba palms at the outer edges of the east side of the city, you can watch Teresina start to come to life. The neighborhood surrounding Frei Serafim Avenue gets an especially early start, a process you might observe when in the company of friends determined to extend their nighttime bohemia into the following day.

© The Author(s) 2019
T. E. Murphy, *Queerly Cosmopolitan*,
https://doi.org/10.1007/978-3-030-00296-1_3

Unless it is a Sunday, you will see numerous buses and vans, small delivery trucks, and a few cars and motorbikes running in both directions along the avenue's tree-lined esplanade. Waiting quietly at the bus stops lining the avenue are domestic workers and other working-class residents who have come from some of the farthest reaches of the city. You will notice men riding old heavy bicycles transporting large plastic water bottles or bins of homemade salty tapioca cakes and thermoses of sweet coffee to be sold on the street downtown. You might see women toting reused paper shopping bags from fancy boutiques, some wearing shin-length skirts—a common requirement for Evangelical women when out in public—and some that have wet, curly hair pulled tight into a ponytail or a bun. You may also notice that many men and women are wearing worn-in and brightly colored Havaiana-style flip-flops and at least one thin colored ribbon tied around their wrist—the latter usually indicating that they are waiting for God, the Virgin Mary, or a saint to grant them a wish. If you walk along the esplanade toward downtown and sit on one of the wooden benches, you will witness a significant transformation take place: the sun and heat will gain force, almost blanching the colorful landscape and the six-lane boulevard, and the esplanade will become increasingly packed with vehicles and pedestrians. You will see buses carrying students and service workers with wet, combed hair, wearing an assortment of uniforms preparing to report for duty throughout downtown. You will also see a number of new cars coming from the distinguished East Zone across the Kubitschek Bridge transporting government employees sporting suits and blouses, medical professionals clad in lab coats, and students wearing uniforms from the city's most established private schools, all of whom on average are taller, paler, and have straighter hair and a more uniform complexion than Teresinenses coursing along the avenue by other means of transportation. As bus stops quickly become crowded and more bicycles and pedestrians populate the esplanade, the energy builds—horns honk, talk becomes louder and more expressive, cars and bicycles blare advertisements from giant speakers, and the military academy band kicks off its morning repertoire. If you watch more closely, you will also see where people are headed: down a side street toward a government office, to another bus stop to take a different bus, to the public hospital, into a gas station, westward into the commercial district toward the Old Market, into a snack shop or bakery for a quick breakfast, to a butcher shop or grocery store, or into one of numerous former gingerbread-style homes of local elites that have been converted into cell phone stores, travel agencies,

Fig. 3.1   Intersection on Frei Serafim Avenue

car dealerships, clinics, and new small private high schools and technical schools (Figs. 3.1 and 3.2).

Frei Serafim remains moderately populated until the lunch hour, when life on the street intensifies yet again, though this time in a different vein. By noon, Teresina's sun and heat are ablaze—hot enough to fry an egg on the sidewalk, the saying goes—and locals become anxious to eat or to get home or both. Buses move with greater thrust, more pedestrians dodge traffic to cross the avenue, and all vehicles on the road are caught in a tense race, a moment that almost always produces an anxious traffic jam for those heading across the bridge to the East Zone (Figs. 3.3 and 3.4).

The East Zone, considered the wealthiest and most sophisticated of Teresina's five sectors, houses the priciest, most modern, and most elaborate commercial establishments and residences. It is where many upwardly mobile Teresinenses live and own businesses; for those who do not, it remains a dream. For most residents who have managed to secure a life that revolves around the East Zone, downtown is the only other

Fig. 3.2   Crowded bus stop on Frei Serafim Avenue

sector of considerable import. Although the majority of such residents consider it anything but sophisticated, downtown cannot be ignored, as numerous activities and services important to upwardly mobile Teresinenses can be found only there. The East Zone, however, did not always outshine downtown in terms of status, nor was it likely that Teresina's earliest urban planners would have ever imagined it would become the city's most prestigious sector.

Locally prided as one of the first cities in Brazil to undergo its initial development by way of urban planning, Teresina's downtown unfolded between the city's two rivers, following a gridiron pattern such that streets heading East and West ran parallel from one river's edge to the other, and parallel streets running North and South bisected them. With its location between the two rivers and with the Parnaíba River serving as the state's western border, the city's options for urban expansion were to the North, South, Southeast, and East, resulting in the city's four other zones (Figs. 3.5 and 3.6).

Fig. 3.3   Cars, trucks, bicycles, and motorcycles heading East on Frei Serafim Avenue

Despite Teresina's scant recognition on a national scale, during the first hundred years of Teresina's existence, downtown was the city's locus of social, political, and economic importance. It was the site for government buildings, cathedrals, schools, the municipal theater, the central market, numerous park-like plazas and homes of the new local elite, most of whom were families of large-scale landowners and cattle ranchers from the countryside. The wide, mansion-lined Frei Serafim Avenue was the most prominent and prestigious avenue during the first half of the twentieth century as it was dominated by elaborate homes of the local elite.

By the second half of the century, the mile-long avenue had become the city's East-West axis, dividing it in two and serving as a corridor to the city's new elite sector on the East side of the Poti River. In the 1960s especially, Teresina and other cities throughout the state began to experience a tremendous amount of population growth, a trend continuing up to the present, though with less intensity in recent years (Fundação

Fig. 3.4   The East Zone

CEPRO 2002: 39). From the 1950s onward, Teresina would become the state's primary center of industry, commerce, universities, technology, and healthcare, requiring a substantial labor force (Fundação CEPRO 2002: 40). Thus, from 1950, when the city's population is estimated to have been around 90,000, in a little over half of a century later it had reached nine times that size, resulting in a population of roughly 800,000 residents in 2009 (Nascimento 2007).

As downtown's population increased, with new residents migrating from the drought-stricken and impoverished countryside, well-to-do families in Teresina who owned land on the east side of the Poti River began developing it and selling lots to families looking to relocate from their downtown homes in search of a more suburban lifestyle. This pattern of elites migrating across the Poti River pressed on over time, depreciating the value of downtown residences and diminishing much of the prestige previously associated with the west side of the Poti River (the Ilhotas neighborhood being the most notable exception). Though the vast major-

Fig. 3.5   The confluence of the rivers Poti and Parnaíba

ity of the city and state's government offices still remain downtown, this mass exodus of elite and upwardly mobile residents to the East Zone transformed downtown from the city's center of prestige to a locus of public and private services and small businesses, many of which today are housed in the former mansions of the local elite (Fig. 3.7).

Although widely considered to be Teresina's most sophisticated zone, the East Zone is anything but uniformly refined. It is indeed home to the vast majority of the city's most expensive, elaborate, and cutting-edge

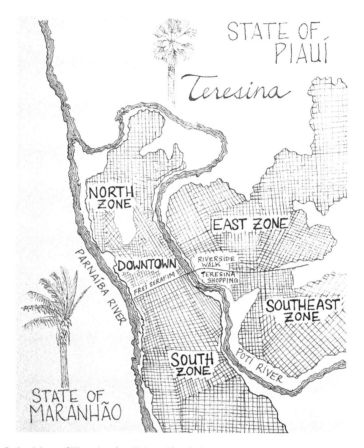

Fig. 3.6 Map of Teresina by Krista Chael, 2018

goods, services, and establishments: the state's only two shopping malls, the vast majority of the city's 20-plus story condominiums, upscale boutiques, designer furniture stores, high-quality grocery stores and bakeries, restaurants serving nonlocal food, foreign language schools, pricy bars and nightclubs, highly reputed schools and universities, and large private security companies. Still, decidedly unsophisticated living conditions, activities, and establishments found in all sectors of the city also populate the East Zone: precariously constructed wattle and daub homes, unpaved dirt roads, abandoned lots and homes in disrepair, brick walls painted with brightly colored advertisements for local businesses, lone mules grazing

Fig. 3.7   Former elite home on Frei Serafim Avenue

on weeds, small modest corner stores, people of all ages riding old bicycles, piles of white plastic grocery bags full of trash placed on curbs outside residences, and men in cowboy hats riding mule-driven carts transporting anything from freshly cut branches to home appliances to materials for recycling, and residential streets made of irregularly shaped rocks that are positioned one next to another, making for slow and bumpy driving (and making walking or biking a formidable challenge—activities that are seldom experienced by the majority of the occupants of such homes). Still, the zone's thoroughfares are among the city's best cared for, cushioning the tires of the majority of the Teresina's most expensive automobiles. In the densest and fanciest segments, houses and the occasional vacant lot sit one next to another, each surrounded by plaster-covered brick walls no less than eight-feet high, crowned with a combination of deterrents for the unwelcome visitor, ranging from broken glass and metal spikes wedged into concrete to the more conventional, two- to three-foot-high electrically charged fence. Condominiums scattered across the zone are thought to be more secure, for in addition to the security measures taken up by private residences, these ultra-modern buildings come with security guards working around the clock (Figs. 3.8, 3.9, 3.10, 3.11 and 3.12).

Fig. 3.8 New condominiums contrast with more modest dwellings

Fig. 3.9 East Zone—condominium construction

Fig. 3.10 East Zone—condominiums positioned next to large single-family homes

From the construction of mansions downtown to the proliferation of condominiums east of downtown, pursuits of sophistication and distinction have shaped Teresina's landscape since its very beginning. Yet the built environment is but one component of the look, feel, and meaning of an urban landscape. As the beginning of this chapter illustrates, people play an equally significant role in how a place is understood and experienced. What follows is a closer look at how people and places in Teresina intersect in the creation of a hot, dynamic, and meaningful somewhere.

Fig. 3.11   East Zone—new condominiums sprouting out of former farmland

Fig. 3.12   Electrically charged fences line the tops of high walls surrounding condominiums

ESCAPING TEREHELL

"It's not going to fall. I promise." André assured me as I slowly slid the large pane of glass along the track. "But what about now? Agh. It just makes me so nervous that it's going to fall out and kill someone down there!" I said. André and Sérgio laughed. "That's not going to happen. Now just slide the wheel out of the track and fold the pane inward toward the wall." "No." I said to André. "You do it first."

André was trying to show me how to open and close the frameless tinted glass windows he recently had installed all along the balcony of his 12th-floor condo in Teresina's East Zone. I would be taking care of his place for about a month while he went on a vacation in Eastern Europe. Sérgio and André are old friends of mine. I met them both back in 2004. Sérgio had long been a central figure in the galera[1]—he's an architect, a designer, and a producer of *festas* (parties). I first met André, Sérgio's cousin, when he was one of my students at the language school. André only occasionally involves himself in the goings-on of the galera. He's not much into nightlife but would make an exception that night. Our mutual friend and architect, Marcelo was throwing a party for his boyfriend's 30th birthday. The three of us had decided to meet at André's condo and go from there.

The new windows on André's balcony essentially allow a person to stack all the glass panes at one end so that it appears as a regular, window-less balcony. This was André's most recent improvement to the condo. He said it would make it possible to sit on the balcony and run the small but potent air conditioner mounted on the wall in the living room. Manipulating the space with glass dividers and ductless "split" air conditioners—as they are popularly called—to keep his home at an ideal temperature was not new for André. Over the five years I had known him, he had enclosed both his home office and the utility area off the kitchen with large glass doors and acquired four different splits for his two-bedroom condo. All these modifications would allow him more options for cooling some areas and not cooling other areas without compromising the open layout of the condo.

---

[1] The "galera" refers to the clique of people who come together to form Teresina's nocturnal bohemia (Chap. 4).

"But if it gets windy," André cautioned as I stepped out the front door to tap the elevator button, "be sure to close them, or they could bang against one another and break." "Seriously?!" I said, incredulous. Chuckling more, he reassured me, "They won't break, but if they do, they will fall inward. I promise."

The elevator was chilly, but not as chilly as the air inside André's new Citroën—the only one of its kind in the whole city, he proudly attested as we exited the compound. Sérgio immediately began to poke fun at André for always trying to appear *chique* (chic) as we headed to Marcelo's house—just 15 minutes from André's place. Sprouting out of the lush vegetation of angélica, babaçu, and carnauba trees was Marcelo's neighborhood—one of Teresina's first large-scale gated communities, its walls and gates standing taller than that of any other residential wall in the city.

Once inside the gates, I was immediately transported. This was not Teresina. Maybe not even Brazil. I couldn't help but take note of how much it looked like a North American suburb, so open and expansive that you didn't even notice the walls—a near impossibility in the rest of the city nowadays. An artificial pond sat at the neighborhood's center. Uniformly cut curbs and sidewalks lined the expanse of grassy front yards. But when I opened the car door, the thickness of the air and the sting of smoke from something burning in the distance pierced my nose and immediately reminded me that I was indeed in Teresina.

Marcelo's home was doubtless the ultramodern white cube-like structure emitting red flashing lights and house beats. Inside, women and men mingled and danced with flutes of champagne in hand. Greeting friends and acquaintances as we went, we worked our way to the backyard where Sérgio had located some of our other friends standing around tall bar tables positioned on high-grade artificial grass. As we stood next to a tree, chatting and sipping our champagne, something felt amiss. When André nudged me to point out a guy he had been crushing on, I turned around, and there it was: a ten-foot-tall industrial-sized air conditioner cooling the first floor *and* the backyard.

CHIQUE DISTINCTION

How Teresinenses deal with the daily heat can serve as a form of social distinction (Bourdieu 1984), a demonstration of privilege, a symbol of how *chique* (chic) a person is. The trajectory of my evening with André and Sérgio—from a partially air-conditioned recently built condominium in Teresina's East Zone, out into a hot hallway, into a chilly mirrored elevator, out into a muggy parking garage, into the freezing blustery air of a new car, out into the thick hot air of a gated community, and then finally into a partially air-conditioned private home—is a common one for a growing class of Teresina's residents. Indeed, André's career as a successful lawyer in his mid-40s with no dependents enables such a lifestyle—one characterized not by a complete escape from the heat, but by the best of what Teresina can offer: a life of fragmented, if partial, climate-controlled escapes. Escaping into climate-controlled microclimates throughout one's day signals an abundance of socioeconomic and physical mobility—a lifestyle of luxury to which many residents aspire.

A similar evening with Nenê—who has no car and pieces together her monthly salary by teaching Spanish classes at a few different schools in different parts of the city—would have yielded a much different trajectory. Although it would not be unheard of for Nenê to be invited to a party like Marcelo's—the galera evidences a rather unusual tendency to include people of various levels of Teresina's large and expanding middle class—it is unlikely she would have gone. Few buses pass by Marcelo's condominium, especially at night, so she would have needed to ride with someone else—a favor normally reserved for family members, close friends, and significant others. And while taxis are technically an option, arriving to such a fancy party in a gated community on the back of a motorcycle taxi is virtually unheard of for someone with aspirations of upward mobility. Alternately, a car taxi ride tends to run two to three times the cost of that of a moto taxi and roughly ten times the cost of a bus ride—a high price for Nenê to pay as the major breadwinner of her household. Therefore, the night would instead have most likely begun downtown in the thick hot air of her humble home where she lives with her mother and sister. It would have either ended there or involved another trajectory altogether—perhaps involving something more in line with her girlfriend Raquel's plans, who, still living at home with her parents, often borrows the family car to go out at night. Nenê's lack of a climate-controlled home or easy access to climate-controlled transport is indicative of her comparative lack of mobility—both socioeconomic and physical—and means she spends more time coping with the heat and less time escaping it. As such, Nenê's life is structured more by surrendering to the climate than controlling it. Which is to say that Nenê represents a different part of Teresina's expanding middle class from that of André despite the fact that residents of all middle-class positions are engaging in new forms of consumption, status performances, and upward mobility more now than ever before.

Teresina's urban transformation is striking, if not disorienting. Over the past 50 years rural-urban migration has made a tremendous impact on the city. With approximately 90,000 residents in 1960, today Teresina is home to more than 800,000 (Nascimento 2007). Combined with this growth, Brazil's recent economic boom and new socioeconomic policies have dramatically altered the look and feel of the city. Between 2003 and 2010, I witnessed dozens of ultramodern, towering condominiums popping up around the malls; new cars flooding the streets; and an increasing number of people standing in lines waiting to purchase all kinds of appliances— from washing machines to laptops to plasma TVs. What I witnessed in Teresina during those years was part of a widespread change taking place not only in the Northeast, but throughout the country: a reshuffling of social positions and the rise of Brazil's new middle class.

In Teresina's dynamic terrain of shifting social positions, demonstrations of social status have become increasingly important for residents' ability to gain a sense of place and belonging in the city. Escaping Teresina's heat, as my evening with André and Sérgio suggests, is a demonstration of one's ability to distance oneself from the hot and poor inevitability of daily life in Teresina. But escaping the heat is just one of many ways that people in Teresina demonstrate their distinction. A close investigation of the local category of distinction—*chique*—offers insight into just how nuanced and important status performances have become in the midst of Teresina's social and cultural transformation. It is by performing one's chique-ness that residents are able to distance themselves from necessity and the ordinary and rub shoulders with that which is considered privileged, extra, and more refined. A lifestyle that often conjures up more than just a whiff of fora.[2]

LITTLE TERESINA

"Before the malls, Teresina seemed so much smaller," Raquel once told me. Raquel went on to explain that this was the case in the past because, for the most part, she and the people she knows were accustomed to find-

---

[2] "*Fora*" (outside) is a term that is often used to signal a particular set of foreign places and cultures imagined to be superior.

ing themselves in social settings where they would see the same faces over and over. During fieldwork, I often heard people remark about how the city's population seemed to have exploded over night—a comment that was often followed up by a discussion of the shopping malls. Housing Teresina's only two cinemas as well as other amenities and consumables available nowhere else in the city, the malls attract residents from all sectors, bringing people in contact with others who, apart from work, had previously seldom left the zone in which they live. Although the malls may have made it seem like Teresina's population multiplied exponentially over night, it did not. Rather, a pervasive shift in terms of opportunities for consumption and patterns of movement more generally changed the face of the city in a relatively short period of time—a dynamic process that continues to transform the city today.

Brazil has five official social classes—A, B, C, D, and E, each of which is measured in terms of the number of minimum wages a household earns per month. While these official categories are one way to think of Brazil's class positions, in popular discourse many Brazilians also rely on the categories of lower, middle, and upper class, complicating many people's understandings of class membership in Brazil. A number of Brazilians I have spoken to, Teresinenses and otherwise, have explained that this confusion over class membership is partly due to Brazil's "new C class" or the "digital middle class" (Barreto 2011). Though comprised of people with a lower household income than those of class A or B, members of class C experience a lifestyle that is much more similar to those of class A or B than ever before. Largely due to greater access to credit and a system of "*parcelas*," where payments for goods and services from shoes to washing machines to vacation packages to cars can be paid for in small monthly installments usually ranging anywhere from 12 to 60 months, class distinctions are becoming increasingly ambiguous. Whereas many members of class C not so long ago would have been considered "lower class," today they lead lives that look very much like those of a more global middle class (Heiman et al. 2012). As such, it is not uncommon for members of all three classes (A, B, and C) to refer to themselves as "*classe média*" ("middle class").

Teresinenses often claim that, overwhelmingly, their city is comprised of two social classes: lower and middle. In 2008, *Classe A* and *Classe B*—the nation's two wealthiest classes—comprised less than 13% of Teresina's entire population. Teresina's *Classe C* comprised 46.5% of Teresina's population, whereas its two poorest classes—*Classe D* and *Classe E*—comprised

40.5% of the city's population (Neri 2009).[3] Teresina's so-called middle class is beginning to feel as ambiguous a category as it does in the US; it includes people that range from maids who ride buses and sell Avon to civil servants, doctors, and small business owners who own more than one car, have second homes in the countryside, and whose children are enrolled in the city's most prestigious private schools.

The result is that while people from lower echelons are moving up in class position and gaining greater physical mobility within and beyond the city, a growing number of residents previously considered "middle class" are becoming less certain about their ability to maintain a position of chique distinction in light of this new middle rising from below. It is becoming less and less obvious who is *truly* sophisticated, wealthy, and powerful, and who is just faking it. Residents whose families wield clout in small towns in the countryside are especially implicated in this quest for chique distinction; in Teresina, where the current population is approximately 800,000, many family names, political ties, and public performances guaranteed to yield prestige in the countryside are diminishing in worth in this growing capital. To be considered among the ranks of Teresina's most upwardly mobile residents, then, these families must work harder for recognition, a process that is highly contingent upon one's ability to perform distinction (Bourdieu 1984).[4]

As one might expect in such a context, consumption practices and public performances of sophistication have become acutely important to residents in their attempts to be seen as wealthy, powerful, and prestigious (Oswald 1999; Beng-Huat 2000, O'Dougherty 1999, Liechty 2003). Typical of people caught in such tense contexts of social repositioning, members of Teresina's middle class commonly ascribe status positions to others and are quick to condemn those who consume and/or partake in practices thought to be inappropriate (Bourdieu 1984; O'Dougherty 1999; Liechty 2003). Many Teresinenses, including participants in the

---

[3] On a scale that rates 36 of Brazil's most populated urban areas, Teresina finds itself at number 17 in terms of its percentage of *classes A* and *B* combined. In contrast, *classes A* and *B* make up 36.48% of the population of Florianopolis, which is in position number 1 (Neri 2009).

[4] Along with Bourdieu (1984), Weber (1946), and others, I share Julie Bettie's position that "there are exceptions to the class-origin-equals-class-performance rule" (Bettie 2003: 50–51). Thus, I take up the local category of *chique* and other local categories of distinction to draw attention to the contested nature of prestige in Teresina.

galera, rely on a number of morally charged distinctions that spill over national categories of class: *"famílias tradicionais"*—families known for their wealth and power,[5] *"famílias tradicionais em decadência"*—once powerful families who are now in economic decline but benefit financially from the reputation of their name, *"burguêsa burocrata"*—bourgeois bureaucrats who often are accused of stealing money from the state both directly and indirectly, and *"novos ricos"*—nouveaux riches living off of credit and/or by exploiting their employees. Although these categories help some residents make sense of where they stand in comparison to other residents, arguably more significant to establishing a sense of belonging in the city are practices of chique distinction.

CHIQUE DISTINCTION: A MATTER OF APPEARANCE

When I first arrived in Brazil, I was immediately struck by how frequently I would hear candid remarks about ugliness that did not always make sense to me. When I expressed my confusion to Mariel, she laughed and uttered unapologetically, "This is Brazil! 'Ugly' means 'poor.' Don't you know the phrase, 'There's no such thing as an ugly woman—only a poor woman' (*'Mulher feia não existe—só tem mulher pobre'*)?" With the right amount of money, Mariel explained, anyone can become beautiful with the help of clothing and any number of "treatments"—from those intended to improve one's complexion, hair texture and color, to others aimed at sculpting an attractive body with medicines, exercise, and surgery.

Keeping up appearances is a not a recent phenomenon in Brazil (e.g., Goldenberg 2007; Edmonds 2010), and attempts to distinguish oneself as wealthier, more prestigious, more powerful, or more fortunate than the next person can be observed in numerous contexts in Teresina. The ubiquitous use of the term, *"chique"* offers much insight into this tendency. Not to be confused with French or American connotations of *chic*, chique can be used to signify virtually any person, place, or thing that is thought to be beyond the necessary, ordinary, or quotidian (Bourdieu 1984). It can point to something extraordinarily beautiful, sophisticated or expensive, or simply impressive.

---

[5] Familias tradicionais often established wealth and power through a long history of exploiting some of the state and nation's poorest residents living in the Northeastern countryside.

I initially found the usage of this word quite peculiar. I recall a secretary at the language school where I worked using it almost constantly. A colleague would stop into the school on his day off wearing a nicely fitted shirt: "*Que Chiiiiiqueeee!*" she would say with an exaggerated, pouty, and a well-aren't-*you*-fancy sort of expression on her face. A student would talk about having recently returned from a trip to the beach with his parents: "*Que Chiiiiiqueeee!*" A teacher would mention how she could not wait for the weekend to arrive as she would spend it swimming in her friends' pool: "*Que Chiiiiiqueeee!*" I began to notice that it was not only she who used the word to characterize a vast assortment of experiences, aesthetics, performances, locations, and objects. Similar to the way that "fancy" became a descriptor for a brand of ketchup in the US, chique can refer to anything from sipping champagne in Paris, to planning an elaborate wedding, to the construction of a franchise from fora, like McDonald's. To be chique is to be better, exceptional, and outstanding.

Like all types of status, what is chique is both relational and hierarchical (Weber 1964; Bourdieu 1984). Teresina's two shopping malls in the greater context of Teresina provide a clear illustration of this. In the late 1990s, Teresina's social life underwent a dramatic shift with the construction of both malls in the East Zone—"Teresina Shopping" and "Riverside Walk."[6] Prior to this moment, this sweltering capital had no expansive public space for pedestrians to stroll, loiter, or gather with some relief from the harsh elements.[7] The two malls—complete with vaulted ceilings, high-powered cooling mechanisms, and numerous spotless spaces for gathering, strolling, eating, drinking, and shopping—revolutionized social life for not only residents of the East Zone, but for thousands of Teresinenses residing in all corners of the city. Because visitors to the malls must eventually return to the comparatively hot, disorganized, less secure, and less fora-looking landscape beyond the malls' gates, whether it be back to work or school downtown or back home to Teresina's other zones, the malls and other aesthetically modern establishments and residences in the East Zone feel especially chique (Figs. 3.13, 3.14, 3.15 and 3.16).

[6] Both names are in their original, English-inspired Portuguese. Perhaps somewhat tellingly in terms of the malls' overwhelming importance to residents, Teresina Shopping is often called "Teresina" for short.

[7] Prior to 1997, Teresina had a few small strip mall-type commercial centers in the East Zone and one covered walkway downtown with fans and misters, but none compared to the expansive internal spaces provided by the two malls.

Fig. 3.13 Shopping mall entrance

Fig. 3.14 Shopping mall interior

Fig. 3.15 Venders selling clothing beneath umbrellas permanently occupy one street downtown

What is chique, then, is relative to the specific context in which it is positioned. Chique's look and feel is also never stable in that it is subject to disagreement and negotiation by those who employ it. Chique might be akin to the outmoded concept of being "in" in the US—for example, being part of the "in" crowd or wearing clothes that are considered "in." What is "in" and what is "out" is only obvious to those who are "in," and different groups have different criteria for what is and what is not "in." That said, a snapshot of the Teresina I experienced during my stay there can offer some insight into what is more and less chique for at least one segment of the population: the expanding, upwardly mobile middle class.

Chique Transport

To even begin to think about being considered chique by the lot of Teresina's most upwardly mobile residents—primarily those whose lives

Fig. 3.16   Downtown—a space of improvisation and bricolage when compared to the pristine controlled environment of the East Zone's shopping malls

revolve around the East Zone—one must first recognize the importance of how people move about the city. It is not only imperative that those aspiring to be chique use a particular mode of transportation but also that they abide by a number of commonsense rules about urban transit in general. What one ought to do is travel by car, ideally one's very own, and preferably an expensive new car. Owning one's own car is of greater importance than owning one's own home in Brazil, and especially given the recent incentives for Brazilians to purchase cars at unprecedentedly low rates,[8] the upwardly mobile have few acceptable excuses for using any other means of transport. But cars are not chique in their own right. Rather, their chique-ness depends upon the prevalence of less sophisticated ways of moving about the city: walking, biking, riding buses, riding motorcycles, and taking motorcycle taxis. Relying on any of these modes of transport suggests one's lack of ability to acquire one's own car. And in a city like Teresina, the extreme daily heat, the lack of infrastructure amenable to pedestrians, bicyclists, and bus riders, as well as the frequent occurrence of armed assaults, few with access to a car would opt for one of these other modes of transport. Countless stories of people staying at home and forgoing attending school, an appointment, or a social event due to their inability to secure a car ride suggests that having a car is about much more than convenience. In Teresina, where the majority of residents still lack access to a car,[9] having one is fundamental to convincing others of one's chique-ness.

Chique Spaces and Performances

Moving about the city appropriately is just the first step in constructing a chique image within Teresina's expanding middle class. *Being* chique means *performing* chique in a number of different contexts. Where, when, and how one shops, eats, exercises, runs errands, hosts or attends special events, and simply socializes must also conform to chique standards.

The only enclosed spaces in Teresina that afford residents the chance to stroll and shop while being protected from the city's intensifying sun, heat, and crime,[10] Teresina's two malls are one of the primary sites for demonstrations of chique-ness. Mall security is ensured by a limited number of entrances, each of which is policed by uniformed security

---

[8] Ford offered interested buyers a down payment of R$1000 and 72 monthly payments of only R$500 (Noticias Automoveis n.d.). One way the Brazilian government attempted to prevent involving itself in the 2009 economic crisis was to stimulate the automotive market. The removal of a 7% import tax on certain models of cars resulted in mass car consumption throughout the country (Kugel 2009). In one month in 2010, Teresina had some of the highest numbers of car sales per capita in the country.

[9] Though the number of cars on Teresina's roads has increased dramatically from 109,811 vehicles registered in 2001 to 317,000 in 2012, the numbers still amount to roughly two cars for every five residents (Humana Saúde 2012).

[10] Though in August of 2011, after I completed fieldwork for my doctoral dissertation, isolated shootings took place inside both shopping malls.

guards, often armed with a pistol, club, and walkie-talkie. The guards' job is to discreetly protect customers while discouraging "rascals" ("*malandros*") from committing crimes in a space where one must pass a security guard upon exiting. Especially for people with something to lose and families with children, this presence of security is quite significant. In a city where the gated community is a relatively recent housing option, the mall is considered one of the most secure spaces in the city where one can socialize, shop, and be entertained. Pristine and orderly, these miniature worlds also speak to many locals' yearnings for a more modern, cosmopolitan, and fora-esque life than what can be obtained elsewhere across Teresina's sprawling, rural, and comparatively chaotic-looking landscape. As such, the malls entice patrons by aiming to fulfill the urban desires of entire families: they play host to indoor playgrounds, secure banking, entire grocery stores, pharmacies, medical facilities, post offices, the city's only two cinemas, department stores, cell phone companies, fashionable clothing stores, top-notch jewelry and perfume stores, chique hair salons, foreign language schools, and bookstores, all of which tend to have higher-quality customer service than a good number of other commercial establishments downtown and throughout the rest of the city. Moreover, like the malls' very names—Teresina Shopping and Riverside Walk—a fair number of establishments make references to languages and cultures associated with fora: Hot Sun, Club Miss, The Toys, Praça do Japão (Japan Plaza), Chili Beans, Beer Store, Blackout, A Cigana (The Gypsy), City Shoes, and Sleep Center.

Performing chique also happens beyond the gates of the malls. In the early morning and in the late afternoon/early evening, just in front of Riverside Walk, chique performers can be found walking and jogging along Raul Lopes Avenue. Whether there or at one of the zone's many high-end air-conditioned gyms, men and women can be found wearing new, sporty brand-name clothes. On average, these bodies working to appear among the city's chique-est tend to be among Teresina's fairest-skinned and most sculpted—resulting from not only family history but also protection from the sun, a nutritious diet, adequate sleep, and a number of artificial enhancements ranging from protein supplements to plastic surgery—all of which are luxuries in Teresina as they require, at the very least, ample time. As such, any type of exercise for the sake of exercise is considered somewhat chique among Teresina's poorest residents, for whom the time and energy to exercise generally implies a certain amount of distance from necessity (Bourdieu 1984).

Convincing demonstrations of chique-ness are highly complex, and when considering the concept of "race," especially as it is understood throughout North America, chique performances appear even less straightforward. In Brazil, "race" is far less of an essential category than it is in the US. Due to a greater prevalence of miscegenation over time, Brazil is understood as having a greater number and variety of combinations of skin tones, eye colors, and hair textures among its population, and it is often the case that racial categories become destabilized by different practices and contexts (e.g., Fry et al. 2007; Sheriff 2002; McCallum 2005). As people move in and out of different contexts, it is not uncommon for their "race" to change. Thus, it becomes difficult to generalize about the role of "race" in relation to effective demonstrations of chique-ness. That said, despite the fact that in almost all contexts in Teresina a variety of skin tones are represented, the most privileged members of society are, on average, lighter in skin tone than the less privileged. Nevertheless, effective demonstrations of chique-ness can dramatically influence others' perceptions of one's "race," and, hence, one's status. The prevalence of women under the age of 50 wearing straight/straightened shoulder-length hair or longer throughout much of the East Zone is one example of how "race" is embedded in chique-ness.

Nightfall ups the ante for chique performances. If there is a time of day when residents take extra care to appear attractive, this is it. Whether it be to attend a wedding celebration, a graduation party, a debutant ball, a concert, a night club or even something as routine as having dinner at a new restaurant, attending a church service, meeting friends at a bar, or strolling through the mall, each offers those wanting to show off their chique-est self the perfect context for doing so.

Largely because lunch has long been Teresinenses' principal meal of the day, eating elaborate dinners at home or at restaurants is also thought to be something of a luxury. Though a few dozen restaurants have served dinner in Teresina for some time, these establishments are quickly multiplying—in the East Zone especially—and are becoming increasingly varied in cuisine and ambiance (e.g., French, Middle-Eastern, Japanese, European, and Asian-inspired). While chique performances among these establishments are somewhat varied, their specific chique character more or less corresponds to the formality and priciness of the restaurant—that is, the more expensive, the more formal the ambiance, the more elaborate the style of dress of the patrons. That said, in all such contexts in the East

Zone, the majority of men and women appear strikingly similar in terms of style of dress. Men of all ages can be seen wearing brand-name pants, shoes, shirts, and short hair, whereas the majority of women wear brand-name dresses, skirts, pants/jeans, shoes, and long, straight/straightened hair (except for middle-aged and older women who tend to wear their hair shorter and curlier). Dining out at these restaurants is considered chique not only because they are costly, located in the chique-est zone, and attended by well-dressed patrons, but also because going out to a sit-down dinner and ordering individual meals is something that the majority of Teresinenses rarely experience. More commonly, residents either eat leftovers from lunch (e.g., beans, rice, and perhaps a small amount of meat), have a broth-based soup made with inexpensive ingredients, or simply have a bit of bread or crackers coupled with a small cup of sweet coffee.

Elaborate wedding celebrations, college graduation parties, and debutant balls, on the other hand, are special occasions that are increasingly enjoyed by a much wider segment of Teresinenses. In the East Zone especially, but in other zones as well, these events often take place at one of the city's banquet halls, offering a different kind of chique experience. Especially because these events have begun to be celebrated by more Teresinenses than ever before, chique performers in the East Zone have taken them to a new level of ostentation. Many employ event producers, including a number of participants in the galera, to transform the air-conditioned halls into chique ambiances with the application of extravagant décor centered on a specific theme. Attendees are expected to dress in their most formal attire and should smile pretty for all photographs as they may appear in the local newspaper's social column or online. Chiqueness at these events is demonstrated largely in degrees of elaboration. The more embellished, the more expensive-looking, or the more cutting edge the theme, décor, attire, entertainment, food and drink, the better it is. Conversely, the less formal, the more impromptu, the more basic, the more borrowed, reused, and inexpensive the look, the less chique it is.

CONCLUSION

Successful performances of chique are contingent upon one's ability to convey one's relative wealth and power to others (Weber 1946; Bourdieu 1984). Whether demonstrating one's ability to maintain a comparatively costly lifestyle (e.g., eating out, driving one's own new car, and wearing expensive new clothing), having the luxury of ample time to enjoy leisure activities (e.g., attending chique bars, clubs, and gyms) and invest in one's professional advancement, earning a salary from one of the city's most respected professions, or simply leading a life that is relatively protected from the harsh elements endemic to Teresina, each experience is considered chique, at least in part because it reveals one's privileged access to a kind of lifestyle that is not available to most Teresinenses.

Chique performances are not only demonstrations of economic wealth; specific symbols of fora bear a significant influence on constructing a chique image because fora points to worlds that are imagined to be wealthier, more powerful, and superior in terms of quality of life. Fora serves as what might be considered a kind of cultural capital (Bourdieu 1984) as it can complement and, in certain instances, outclass other more traditional expressions of power. For those who cannot rely on money, a family name, and political affiliations alone for prestige and power—which is the case for the vast majority of Teresinenses—approximating fora in ways acceptable to the upwardly mobile masses can be an alternate route for acquiring chique status.

Especially with increased access to various forms of credit, all kinds of foreign imports and imitation foreign imports—from words to cars to fashions to electronics—have begun to wreak havoc on Teresina's local economy of chique. While in some circles it is enough to display one's connection to the US and Europe by wearing clothing stamped with conspicuous designer names and symbols or English writing, demonstrating one's knowledge of an American or British rock band, or knowing a few words or phrases in English, in other circles—and this appears to be the growing trend throughout Teresina—such demonstrations of one's proximity to fora are too commonplace to confer chique status. Nowadays, one need not spend very much money to acquire a shirt with words and phrases like "Diesel," "California Surfing," or "Stylish Fashion" written across the front. As a result, performing one's proximity to fora in the most upwardly mobile circles means approximating a particular set of outside worlds that Brazil (largely through national media) has recently deemed exotic, beautiful, and on the verge of modern and powerful. For example, Indian-inspired fashions and group excursions to Dubai have recently appeared on the scene—perhaps due to a national telenovela that reified orientalist images of Indian women as exotic, sensual, and beautiful and Dubai as an up-and-coming glamorous cosmopolitan city. Other examples include: learning Chinese (considered chique especially around the time of the Beijing Olympics), donning a soccer shirt referencing the World Cup in South Africa, and going on excursions to Buenos Aires, Argentina, or Santiago, Chile to enjoy a taste of "Europe in South America"—that is, "cold" weather, café culture, fine wines, and other symbols of fora.

Though a good portion of Teresinenses are enjoying greater access to symbols of fora and are beginning to move into some of the chique-est parts of the city, attend some of the chique-est social events, and be seen sporting some of the chique-est fashions, other segments are becoming increasingly uncertain and insecure about their social position. As Teresinenses in general are gaining more exposure to media and are being given more opportunities to travel, many are beginning to see themselves less in terms of the countryside hometowns from which they hail or their immediate neighbors in Teresina, and more in terms of their entire city. In other moments, Teresinenses understand themselves more in terms of the larger spheres of region, nation, and world.

The more residents understand their experiences of be-longing in relation to more distant populations, the more residents tend to question their ability to measure up on a global scale. At one end of the spectrum, some residents appear to be obsessed over anything that hints at fora, while at the other end of the spectrum, other residents attempt to reject fora all together out of fear that their "local culture" will become extinct. Yet what is more common is somewhere in between these two extremes: residents who are drawn to some but not all things associated with fora.

The real power of chique, then, is that for those already endowed with money/power, performances of chique can help to maintain it, while for those without much money/power, chique performances offer possibilities for becoming wealthier/more powerful. The rub, however, is that what is chique and what is not is always changing and, thus, is often understood differently by different residents. What may be the epitome of chique in one setting may be passé or too "gringo"/foreign in another, and as is the case with all performances, not all displays of chique-ness are convincing. Still, not every member of Teresina's middle class relies on chique to distinguish herself from others to establish a sense of be-longing. Some, including many participants in the galera, attempt to reject the economy of chique altogether. This is the subject of my next chapter.

References

Barreto, Jamille. 2011. Brazil Goes Social: The Rise of the Brazilian Digital Middle Class. *Sparksheet*, June 30, 2011. http://sparksheet.com/brazil-goes-social-the-rise-of-the-brazilian-digital-middle-class/

Beng-Huat, Chua, ed. 2000. *Consumption in Asia: Lifestyles and Identities: The New Rich in Asia*. London/New York: Routledge.

Bettie, Julie. 2003. *Women Without Class: Girls, Race, and Identity*. Berkeley: University of California Press.

Bourdieu, Pierre. 1984. *Distinction: A Social Critique of the Judgment of Taste*. Cambridge: Harvard University Press.

Edmonds, Alexander. 2010. *Pretty Modern: Beauty, Sex, and Plastic Surgery in Brazil*. Durham: Duke University Press.

Fry, Peter, Yvonne Maggie, and Marchos Chor Maio, eds. 2007. *Divisões Perigosas: Políticas Raciais no Brasil Contemporâneo*. Rio de Janeiro: Civilização Brasileira.

Fundação CEPRO. 2002. *Piauí: Visão Global*. Teresina: Fundação CEPRO.

Goldenberg, Mirian. 2007. *O Corpo como Capital: Estudos Sobre Gênero, Sexualidade e Moda na Cultura Brasileira*. São Paulo: Estação das Letras e Cores.

Heiman, Rachel, Carla Freeman, and Mark Liechty, eds. 2012. *The Global Middle Classes: Theorizing through Ethnography*. Santa Fe: School for Advanced Research Press.

Humana Saúde. 2012. Número de carros de Teresina triplica em 10 anos. http://humanasaude.com.br/novo/materias/2/n-mero-de-carros-de-teresina-triplica-em-10-anos_20541.html. Accessed 23 Jan 2018.

Kugel, Seth. 2009. Brazil's Message: Buy Now. *Global Post*, June 4, 2009. https://www.pri.org/stories/2009-06-04/brazils-message-buy-now

Liechty, Mark. 2003. *Suitably Modern: Making Middle-class Culture in a New Consumer Society*. Princeton: Princeton University Press.

McCallum, Cecilia. 2005. Racialized Bodies, Naturalized Classes: Moving through the City of Salvador da Bahia. *American Ethnologist* 32 (1): 100–117.

Nascimento, Francisco Alcides do. 2007. Cajuína e Cristalina: as transformações espaciais vistas pelos cronistas que atuaram nos jornais de Teresina entre 1950 e 1970. *Revista Brasileira de Historia* 27 (53): 195–214.

Neri, Marcelo. 2009. *Atlas do Bolso do Brasileiro*. Rio de Janeiro: FGV/IBRE, CPS.

Noticias Automoveis. n.d. Prazo a perder de vista: Ford lança plano de financiamento em 72 meses!!. https://www.noticiasautomotivas.com.br/prazo-a-perder-de-vista-ford-lanca-plano-de-financiamento-em-72-meses/. Accessed 23 Jan 2018.

O'Dougherty, Maureen. 1999. The Devalued State and Nation: Neoliberalism and the Moral Economy Discourse of the Brazilian Middle Class, 1986–1994. *Latin American Perspectives* 104 (2): 151–174.

Oswald, Laura R. 1999. Culture Swapping: Consumption and the Ethnogenesis of Middle-Class Haitian Immigrants. *Journal of Consumer Research* 25 (4): 303–318.

Sheriff, Robin. 2002. Comos Os Senhores Chamavam: Os escravos: discursos sobre cor, raça e racismo num morro carioca. In *Raça como Retorica: a Construção da diferença*, ed. Yvonne Maggie and Claudia Barcellos Rezende, 213–243. Rio de Janeiro: Civilização Brasileira.

Weber, M. 1946. Class, Status, Party. In *From Max Weber: Essays in Sociology*, ed. H.H. Gerth and C.W. Mills, 180–195. New York: Oxford University Press.

Queerly Cosmopolitan

CHAPTER 4

Nocturnal Bohemia

Abstract The chapter opens the second part of the book by presenting Teresina's nocturnal bohemia. Unlike bohemia that are associated with particular neighborhoods, nocturnal bohemia takes place at night in changing locations and is forged around a shared affinity for novel aesthetics and a sense of be-longing to distant worlds. Through an examination of bohemians' shared ethos of queerness around identity and community (e.g., fluidity, flexibility, and openness), the chapter focuses on what happens when outsiders with a fascination and appreciation for unconventional ways of life claim a place for themselves in a city like Teresina. The chapter sheds light on this alternative community's unique orientation to the city and argues that queerness offers a way to conceptualize its cosmopolitan be-longing within the world at large.

Keywords Bohemia • Queerness • Cosmopolitanism • Belonging

Up to now, this book has focused on how the experience of be-longing comes about in the transforming provincial city of Teresina. In different ways, both Chaps. 2 and 3 demonstrate the complex ways in which urban life and the imagination—with the help of technology, the circulation of stories, and increased access to distant worlds—structure residents' sense of self in relation to one another and the world. These chapters have focused on the relationship between the experience of being "local"—living in a

T. E. Murphy, *Queerly Cosmopolitan*,
https://doi.org/10.1007/978-3-030-00296-1_4

place with a widespread reputation for being backward and unimportant—
and the ways in which an imagined superior outside world (*fora*) combined
with demonstrations of *chique* (chic) distinction structures that experience.
Now I turn more closely to the galera,[1] exploring how its participants
develop community and a sense of be-longing distinct from the city's
upwardly mobile masses.

QUEERNESS AS BE-LONGING

What sets the galera's be-longing apart from other modes outlined in previous chapters is a certain queerness. A queerness that is both desired and
practiced. Here and throughout the book, my use of "queerness" does not
refer to the popular employment of "queer" as an umbrella term for the
LGBT community. Instead, I rely on two other notions of queerness. On
the one hand, the galera's ethos of queerness refers to shared identifications with alternative and nonnormative ways of life existing at the margins
of mainstream society be they explicitly related to alternative articulations
of gender/sexuality or otherwise (e.g., McCallum and Tuhkanen 2011;
Halberstam 2005). By collectively cultivating a life around avant-garde and
unconventional aesthetics, practices, and perspectives—a process that takes
shape through various types of events, projects, and interactions—the galera maintains itself as a community centered on an interest in the unfamiliar, the novel, and the strange. On the other hand, the galera's queerness
refers to its approach to constructions of self and community—both of
which are conceived of as unbound, in flux, and flexible, unencumbered by
notions that identities are stable or essential (e.g. Allison 2001). Rather
than taking a person's gender/sexuality, socioeconomic status, profession,
self-presentation, or social affiliations to be essential or core characteristics
of the self, the galera largely follows what might be described as "a critical
antiessentialist line of thinking" (McCallum and Tuhkanen 2011: 3),[2] in
which such characteristics are conceived of as positions people take up,

---

[1] The "galera" refers to the clique of people who come together to form Teresina's nocturnal bohemia.

[2] E.L. McCallum and Mikko Tuhkanen point out that this paradigm shift in understanding
identity is "a philosophical scaffolding through which queer theory, impelled not only by
Foucault but by deconstructionist critiques of identity and feminist contestations of con-
stricting definitions of sexual differences, emerged out of a critique of Western metaphysics
and its stable ontology" (2011: 3).

embody, and enact in specific moments under particular contexts (Butler 1990). Espousing a similar notion of identity, Anne Allison (2001), drawing on the work of Lee Edelman (1995), asserts:

> desire and identity always "exceed" (in being more ambiguous and complicated than) the names/categories by which they are routinely slotted. In queerness, the fictive borders demanded by straight society are refused rather than acquiesced to, and excesses (of body/sexuality/gender/subjectivity) are accepted.

In other words, people are always more than labels and no amount of words could ever fully represent who people are and what people desire. Queerness, then, is something that acknowledges and allows for this—an openness to new experiences and the possibility of becoming something other than what dominant society allows.

As a community, the galera is similarly fluid, dynamic, multifaceted, and hard to pin down not only in terms of an identity category but also in space and time. Rather than a community rooted in a particular geographical location, the galera operates in a space of flux where participants connect to one another via social interactions in numerous and changing contexts both in person and via technology.

In recent years, queer theorists have developed the notion of queer time and space under several different yet related rubrics. Some scholars have mobilized the concept of queer time to refer to the rejection of conventional emphases on the future and longevity (McCallum and Tuhkanen 2011; Dean 2009; Bersani 1996; Edelman 1998). Judith Halberstam (2005) formulates queer time and space as those forms of life that arise in the face of the norms that perpetuate "historical living" (McCallum and Tuhkenan 2011: 5). Halberstam elucidates:

> Queer uses of time and space develop, at least in part, in opposition to the institutions of family, heterosexuality, and reproduction. They also develop according to other logics of location, movement, and identification. (2005: 1)

If queerness may be understood in such a way—as an ongoing unconventional relationship to the world or as a process of "becoming" (McCallum and Tuhkanen 2011: 10) rather than "an essential definition of homosexual embodiment" (Halberstam 2005: 6)—the galera may not only offer up a unique embodiment of queerness but of queer time and space as well.

policy closing bars impacted galera (handwritten annotation)

GOOD NIGHT TERESINA

After completing one year of teaching English in Teresina, I left in May 2004 and did not return until June 2006. During my absence, the city government implemented a policy called Good Night Teresina (*Boa Noite Teresina*), mandating that all bars and nightclubs close by 2 am and that alcohol not be sold anywhere in the city until the following day. The policy was intended to eliminate rampant crime in the city—in particular, various types of armed assaults including carjacking. By doing away with late-night opportunities for sociality, fewer people would be on the streets, officials said, and thus, there would be less crime. Though its overall effect on crime was debated, Good Night Teresina most certainly impacted the galera.

In my summers off during graduate school, I returned to Teresina and found that something about the galera was tangibly different. While its community had for some time regularly manifested as an integrated whole around nighttime encounters at concerts, bars, and large *festas* (parties) in changing and inconspicuous locales not normally considered chique, this was no longer the case. A number of bars we had frequented in 2004 had closed, elaborate all-night festas were no longer taking place, and my friends lamented how seldom they were going out compared to before Good Night Teresina. But the galera persisted, largely taking shape around smaller gatherings, sometimes at bars but increasingly at homes. As many as a dozen friends would convene at the house or apartment of one of our few friends who lived alone or another whose parents were out of town for the weekend. We would arrive with CDs, smokes, and cold beers in hand, and spend our evenings sharing music, humorous stories, gossip, musings about potential future social events, art projects, artistic business opportunities, and visions of the future in terms of technology, sociality, and natural resources. Deejays would play mixes they compiled from music they downloaded online, and hosts would update the rest of us on their most recent projects, from home decorations to paintings to crafts made of garbage to home modifications to graphic designs, sketches, and fashions. With the Internet's growing importance, more and more we would find ourselves gathered around a computer, sharing images, YouTube videos, new music, and sometimes entire films. And while small intimate gatherings like these have always been a structuring element of the galera, during the initial years of Good Night Teresina, they were at its center, adding fuel to the galera's fire to dream, experiment, and create.

During these quieter years, the galera began to develop new projects that proved to be extremely important to the community at the time of my fieldwork in 2009 and 2010 when Good Night Teresina was seldom enforced. Like most galera events in the past, two new festas—"Rogues" and "High Jinks: uma festa para todos" ("High Jinks: a party for all")—relied on specific types of transformations that spoke to participants' desire for novelty. Especially in its early days, Rogues carefully invested in creating a different theme for each week, denoted by original flyers, a variety of music (different rock bands and deejays playing a wide range of music), and hence, a varied public, whereas High Jinks—occurring once every few months and often in different locales—brought fans of rock and electronic music together in the same space around a unique theme with corresponding flyers and décor. Bazarro, attempting to circumvent Good Night Teresina, was a monthly bazaar that took place on Sundays at dusk at an abandoned house-turned-punk bar that showcased independent films, electronic and rock music, and works made by artists and artisans from the galera. Bazarro brought together painters and graffiti artists, film buffs, rockers, people with an itch to dance, designers, and people interested in buying locally designed and crafted merchandise. Though it lasted a short six months, Bazarro would prove to be highly influential in the coming years. A few men and women involved would eventually go on to start their own businesses, selling their own creations as well as merchandise they acquired in other cities, and two of them eventually opened their own store in the East Zone, selling hip t-shirts and accessories, toy art, and an assortment of kitsch. While it would be shortsighted to posit Good Night Teresina as entirely responsible for the formation of these new projects, the policy did anything but stifle the galera's creativity, eventually resulting in the galera's return to Teresina's night.

A BOHEMIA OF A DIFFERENT ILK

The galera regularly carves out a special time and space for itself—a form of sociality I call "nocturnal bohemia." Spatially and temporally fragmented—taking place only at night and in changing locations and environments—nocturnal bohemia is where the galera momentarily manifests as an integrated whole. Rather than establishing a bohemia that is fixed in a specific area of the city, then, the galera's bohemia crops up in the night in various and often unfamiliar locales.

Bohemia and the bohemian lifestyle are far from new and are often attributed to a trend taken up by artists in mid-nineteenth-century Paris. In her book, *Bohemians: The Glamorous Outcasts,* Elizabeth Wilson writes:

They were a new race of nomads, whose wandering life from attic to attic, and moonlight flits to avoid paying rent, made them seem like the popular stereotype of gypsies. Like gypsies they moved outside the normal restrictions of society; like gypsies they dressed with ragged flamboyance; like gypsies they rejected honest toil and thrift, preferring to live on their wits; and, just as the gypsies scraped by living by the exploitation of their suspect skills as fortune-tellers, confidence-tricksters, entertainers and even magicians, so new bands of writers and painters produced artefacts that seemed incomprehensible and therefore alarming, often immoral and sometimes disturbingly magical. (Wilson 2000: 21)

Wilson's depiction of the bohemian is prototypical—unconventional, underground, anti-capitalist, artistically productive, sharp, and shabbily chic. Though Wilsons's portrayal of bohemians includes their tendency to roam, bohemian communities of both past and present are often synonymous with particular neighborhoods—specifically those in which rent is inexpensive and establishments cater to the unconventional—for example, Paris' Montparnasse, New York's Greenwich Village, Berlin's Mitte, Chicago's Wicker Park, Rio de Janeiro's Santa Teresa and Zona Sul, and New Orleans' Bywater (e.g., Lause 2009; Levin 2010; Wilson 2000; Graña and Graña 1990; Chauncey 1994; Lloyd 2006; Velho 2002). Although nighttime typically marks a special moment for the bohemian spirit to flourish in such neighborhoods, these sectors are not only bohemian at night. Bohemians live in these neighborhoods and frequent specific establishments around the clock, contributing to the neighborhoods' bohemian reputation. While participants in the galera share a number of characteristics in common with other bohemia in different places and times, the galera's configuration represents a queering of bohemia by being neither a permanent nor an easily identifiable fixture on Teresina's landscape.

Manifesting at night in a wide range of locales, this spatially and temporally mutable bohemia is not restricted to any one sector of the city. It is fragmented, partial, and dynamic; so much so that it goes unrecognized by the vast majority of Teresinenses.[3] Despite the city's sizeable population

---

[3] By and large, the galera's nocturnal bohemia is unrecognized by Teresina's mainstream society. The lack of a fixed name and place with which one might identify the galera and its bohemia makes it difficult to distinguish it as a community. The only term I have heard participants consistently use to refer to their network-community is "galera," which literally means "clique" in Brazilian Portuguese and is commonly used by Brazilians throughout the country to vaguely refer to an intimate group of friends.

and relatively low cost of living, no specific neighborhood in Teresina caters to artists, musicians, and the like to gather for leisure, work, or housing. As such, seldom are artists and bohemians from cities of comparable size tempted to relocate to Teresina for its alternative scene. In the absence of a bohemian neighborhood, members of the galera and other residents pursuing artistic and unconventional lifestyles tend to live in homes scattered around the city. One reason is Teresinenses' reliance on familial support for housing: most people reside with relatives until marriage and/or relocate to housing that is partly financed by family members. Few single people live alone and even less often do friends share housing. Without the conditions for a bohemia to emerge in a specific area of the city, then, establishing an alternative community occurs differently.

Though nighttime provides many Teresinenses a break from the hot hustle and bustle of the workday, it serves the galera with something more: a shared sense of refuge from the normalizing gaze of Teresina's upwardly mobile masses. And while the neighborhood has proved a central feature to the very notion of "bohemia" since the term was first appropriated as such in mid-nineteenth-century France, the importance of a "bohemian spirit," or *la vie bohème*, cannot be overstated. It is this queer sensibility and queer relationship to time and space that marks the galera and its nightlife as unique.

Reviving Nocturnal Bohemia

A couple of months after my arrival for fieldwork in 2009, I set up an interview with Bruno, the producer of Rogues. At the time, Rogues was one of the events most central to the galera; I wanted to learn how it began. On the evening of the interview, Bruno suggested that we meet at Riverside mall.

I spotted Bruno at the entrance right away. He stood out from the rest with his big curly hair, beard, ripped jeans, a fluorescent green and orange t-shirt, and numerous bracelets. He greeted me with a smile and a hug and explained that he had just gotten out of work at the new business that he and a few friends from the university were trying to get off the ground. Bruno recently had quit his job at a large advertising firm and, not worried about paying room and board while living at home with his parents in the South Zone, he was using up the small amount of money he was earning from producing Rogues to contribute to starting the Innovation Workshop

(*Oficina de Inovação*). Different from an agency that single-handedly develops an advertising scheme for a company, theirs attempts to encourage a creative dialogue between agents and clients, helping small business owners realize their visions in such a way that will allow their businesses to flourish. Bruno mentioned two inspirations for the agency: a company located in Rio de Janeiro that he read about online and the short-lived monthly bazaar, Bazarro, that Sérgio had initiated a few years prior at Fabio's punk bar.

As we headed into the air-conditioned food court, Bruno suggested we have a beer at the small bar just inside the door. Cramped, shallow, and drab, with only five small tables and a counter, the bar had never caught my attention before; Bruno remarked with a chuckle that there was no better spot for our interview as it had been instrumental to the creation of Rogues. He explained that he and his friends used to hang out there all because of an online community they created on the social networking site Orkut.[4] As Internet access increased throughout the city in the early 2000s—not only with PCs but also the opening up of numerous Internet cafés—people increasingly used email, Orkut, and MSN Instant Messenger (IM) to keep in touch at a cheaper rate than cell phones. A number of other friends in the galera told me that at that time, through Fotolog and Orkut especially, people would see each others' photos online, exchange a message or two, and become acquainted before meeting in person.

Because Teresina's options for listening to the music that he and his friends liked were limited, the online community served as a space to catalog establishments that they found around town where they could have some drinks and play their own CDs and, in some instances, even their own instruments. Ultimately, the point was to secure a cool place to bring people together, Bruno explained. For the most part, these friends were people he had met at the university and through performing in his indie-rock band. Offline, the community largely revolved around small informal bars located in the East Zone and downtown.

---

[4] Launched in 2004, the same year as Facebook, Orkut was a Google–owned and operated social networking site widely used in Brazil. Like Facebook, Orkut was created to help people maintain and create social relationships through public posts of photos, videos, announcements, and had the feature of sending private messages. In 2006 most everyone I knew in Teresina had an Orkut account, but by 2009, few participants in the galera used their Orkut accounts and instead spent more time on Twitter and Facebook.

When I asked Bruno how Rogues developed out of this community, he told me it all began with Armazém—one of Teresina's few gay, or "*GLS*," bars. *GLS* is an acronym that came out of an identity politics movement to institutionalize gay spaces in Brazil as not exclusively "*Gay*" or "*Lesbica*," but also "*S*," standing for "sympathizers" (*"simpatizantes"*). In Teresina and in much of the country, despite the term's intended politics of incorporating alternative sexualities and affections into heteronormative society through the inclusion of "*S*," these spaces are frequented mostly by self-identified *gays*, *lesbicas*, and trans people as well as others pursuing same-sex affections and sexual practices. It is for this reason that many today say that "GLS" is just another word for "gay."

Armazém, meaning "warehouse," followed a long trend of disguising Teresina's few and often short-lived gay bars with names of radically different types of establishments so attendees could speak about them in mixed company without outing themselves. Some other examples are body shops, factories, and universities. Although Bruno had not been one to frequent GLS bars previously, he was dating a guy at the time who liked to hang out there.

> We would go there about once a week after work, roll and smoke a joint outside, and then go in. At that time, they played only tribal and house music and the clientele was quite gay. Though it wasn't always the case, by 2006 when Rogues began, alternative groups were pretty divided in the city: there were a couple of places in the East Zone for the rockers and there were a couple of gay bars and gay parking lot parties downtown that would play only gay dance club music. There really wasn't anywhere in Teresina that was mixed, where both alternative rock and dance music and their people would mix together.

In 2006, about one year after Armazém first opened and Good Night Teresina was implemented, Teresina's only other gay bar downtown was closing, and, as a result, not much of anything was happening at night downtown. The Orkut community brought together a new combination of musicians, deejays, and friends that would become the very first phase of Rogues. By word of mouth, and the circulation of photos and flyers on Orkut and Fotolog, the word quickly spread to fans of electronic and rock music, forming a community that was mixed not only in terms of music, but also style of dress, social standing, sexual orientation, and gender presentation.[5] Bruno and many of his friends came into contact with numerous people that I had come to know back in the galera's rave days. A new twist on the galera's nocturnal bohemia and its queer form of belonging began to take shape.

Armazém was a small old house in the heart of downtown. When Rogues first started, each Thursday night the checkered dance floor would sweat, covered with a crowd of men and women dancing, flirting, and bonding over shared highs from the music, mind-altering substances, and collective effervescence. Tightly packed together in an orange room off the back of the bar were a host of others hoping to catch a breeze through the windows. The owners eventually expanded the bar, making it nearly three times its original size, and Bruno convinced the owner to allow him to start producing the event by proposing that if he and his friends would be allowed just one night to play their music, they would attract an entirely different public. "He said 'ok,'" booked Rogues for Thursday nights, and look where it is today!" Bruno told me. When I asked him to explain what he meant by "entirely different public," he told me:

> It's really more about the type of music that is played I guess. Friday is definitely GLS, but Thursday is not specific, but it's funny because people that go on Thursday end up going on other nights not knowing it's different and end up liking those nights too! See, if you go on Thursday it doesn't mean anything about your sexuality—no one could say you were gay for going there. On Thursday there's no prejudice about who is there. And it's only five *reais*[6] to get in. I don't think there is any other nightclub in Teresina where someone can go for that cheap.

Participants central to the galera of both past and present point to Rogues as a significant turning point for the galera and its nocturnal bohemia.

---

[5] Rogues brought together clothing styles as diverse as young women wearing tight pants, t-shirts and short hair (a rarity in the city at the time), women with long curly hair wearing loosely fitting dresses and "hippy" jewelry, men with short hair wearing fitted t-shirts and pants emphasizing their muscles, and men with long/shaggy hair and beards wearing loose-fitting clothing.

[6] "Reais" is the plural form of "*Real*," the Brazilian currency.

During a period of time when the galera's social life had become extremely limited in terms of spaces for socializing, Rogues carved out a queer place and time that brought people together who previously were separated by musical taste, sexual orientation, gender presentation, social standing, and neighborhood of residence. As this new galera began to form, other events started to come about (Figs. 4.1, 4.2, 4.3, 4.4 and 4.5).

Fig. 4.1   An otherwise desolate downtown outside Armazém

Fig. 4.2 Nocturnal bohemia—Fabio's punk bar

Fig. 4.3 Nocturnal bohemia—deejay

Fig. 4.4   Nocturnal bohemia—movement

BE-LONGING THROUGH BOHEMIA

Though it has transformed over time, a nocturnal bohemia is not new for the galera. Especially according to its more seasoned participants, this specific configuration of bohemia—manifesting at night in changing and inconspicuous locales—dates back as far as the early 1990s. Nocturnal bohemia was much smaller then and was centered on festas like one called "The End of the Official Trend" ("O Fim da Tendência Official") that took place in abandoned clubs and empty warehouses downtown that were easier to reach via public transportation than many bohemian events in recent years. Another significant change is that whereas Rogues largely relied on the distribution of flyers via online social networks to bring people together, before the arrival of the Internet in Teresina in 1997, the galera depended on other means of advertising that are still practiced today: distributing flyers at bars, stores, and events and by word of mouth. While this nocturnal bohemia has undergone numerous transformations

Fig. 4.5   Nocturnal bohemia—High Jinx

over time, what allows long-standing participants to trace this social world's origins to the not-so-recent past are not only the continued involvement of particular people, but perhaps, more importantly, a shared ethos rooted in queerness.

Consistent with bohemia in other places and times, the galera opens up a unique relationship to time and space in Teresina—a place where people embody lifestyles that are otherwise nonexistent or unacceptable in everyday life. An escape from the pervasive social pressure to conform to the status quo, it is a queer time and space to appropriate and embody ways of life that are imagined to be legitimate if not celebrated elsewhere. As such, nocturnal bohemia takes shape around three intersecting themes at the very core of the galera's ethos: experimentation and novelty; alternative understandings of gender/sexuality; and an ambivalent relationship to "bourgeois" society.

Experimentation and Novelty

Like Rogues, where people are given the chance to test their talent as dee-jays, to listen to unfamiliar music, to move their bodies independently and collectively in new ways, and to try out new perceptions, affections, and self-presentations, the opportunity to lose oneself and experiment in a variety of ways has been an important theme not only for the galera's bohemia but bohemia more generally. In his book, *The Antebellum Crisis and America's First Bohemians*, Mark A. Lause provides a telling quote by Jane McElhenney, a.k.a. "Ada Clare."

> The Bohemian is by nature, if not by habit, a cosmopolite, with a general sympathy for the fine arts, and for all things above and beyond convention. The Bohemian is not, like the creature of society, a victim of rules and customs; he steps over them with an easy, graceful joyous unconsciousness, guided by the principles of good taste and feeling. Above all others, essentially, the Bohemian must not be narrow minded; if he be, he is degraded back to the position of mere worlding. (Lause 2009: 1)

In *Gay New York*, George Chauncey describes the early twentieth century's "Village Bohemia" as having had a "reputation for tolerating nonconformity (or 'eccentricity') and the impetus for social experimentation," and offering a "safe and congenial place for homosexuals to live" (1994: 229). For the galera, experimentation and a love for the novel means collectively challenging a wide range of conventions, an ethos evidenced in names of events like, "Rogues." The name "Rogues," Bruno told me, was inspired by the notion of disrupting the norm, "*quebrar tudo*" ("breaking everything"), much like a rogue. Experimentation involves appropriating new and unlikely spaces throughout the city for bohemian events. The galera's festas, concerts, and performances, for example, often take place in areas and neighborhoods thought to be dangerous, inappropriate for one's class position, or just unusual given the little people know about them. Large plots of land on the outskirts of town, abandoned houses,

empty warehouses, the old train station, a gay bar, and a variety of establishments on the verge of going under are all examples of the kinds of
spaces where the galera's nighttime bohemia comes into being.
Experimentation at events like Rogues, High Jinks, and Bazarro means
sampling and enjoying cutting-edge electronic music, indie-rock, hip-hop,
Brazilian *funk*,[7] *brega*[8] and related genres in the presence of others who
like to do the same. It also means appropriating and inventing fashions
inspired by aesthetics linked to imagined elsewheres—hairstyles, tattoos,
accessories (glasses, shoes, bracelets, etc.), and clothing with specific types
of cuts, designs, and colors. Experimentation at festas means to collectively let go, if temporarily, of local conventions around the body and
mind in general, meaning being receptive to unfamiliar sensations, perceptions, and bodily practices whether induced by mind-altering substances
or the pervasive climate of improvisation that ensues in bohemia.

As I illustrated in the previous chapter, keeping up appearances among
Teresina's growing middle class leaves little room for deviations from the
norm in daily life, whether in terms of how one moves about the city, what
one wears, and where one is seen and with whom. Nocturnal bohemia,
then, carves out an alternate relationship to time and space whereby people can try out new aesthetics and sociality with few concerns about risking
one's reputation in the eyes of mainstream society.

Alternative Understandings of Gender and Sexuality

As Chauncey (1994), Lause (2009), and Brown (1985) point out, such
contexts of bohemian experimentation also provide a space for alternative
views about gender and sexuality to flourish. Indeed, nonnormative
expressions of gender/sexuality have always been part of the nocturnal
bohemia: women and men donning attire, dancing, and interacting with
others in ways not normally considered appropriate for their respective
genders (which is always a specific intersection of "race," class, age, and
social status). And while a great many participants in the galera engage in
same-sex sexual practices and relationships, a fair number do not. As

[7] Brazilian funk, or *funk Carioca* (funk from Rio de Janeiro), is a genre of music in Brazil
that was inspired by Miami bass and freestyle. It is associated with favela life in Rio and is
often criticized for objectifying women through lyrics and its culture in general.
[8] Widely used throughout Brazil, "brega" generally refers to older music (1960s onward)
considered to be overly sentimental, romantic, and, hence, humorous.

Bruno's comments suggest, something more pervasive than same-sex attraction seems to underpin the community.

For most participants in the galera, Teresina's gay subculture is distinct from their nocturnal bohemia. There are "gay festas" and there are "galera festas." Between 2003 and 2010, I attended numerous GLS bars, clubs, and festas, and learned more than a little bit about the increasing presence of LGBT social organizations and identity politics on the local landscape. The galera and its nocturnal bohemia differ from many LGBT events in a few important ways. Teresina's nocturnal bohemians are generally less sepa-rated along lines of gender and sexual orientation, and while single people of various ages are common to both spheres, they seem to place less empha-sis on sex and sexual identity (e.g., finding someone to hook up with for the night, and engaging in discussions that reference gay/lesbian identity and a sense of belonging to a larger imagined gay community).[9] In other words, taking part in the nocturnal bohemia seldom entails listening to deejays play exclusively "gay" music or engaging in talk of romance and sexuality to the extent that people with opposite-sex and/or ambiguous sexual desires might feel excluded. It is as if the presence of a more normative LGBT community in Teresina has allowed the galera to construct commu-nity along lines other than gender and sexuality. Instead, what brings the galera together is a shared passion for experimenting with novel aesthetics and creating ways of life that are not present in everyday local life. As such, nocturnal bohemia carves out a space where people can be relatively open with one another about their same-sex desires without their involvement in the galera being attributed to their same-sex desires. While select members of the galera support the LGBT community through their expertise as dee-jays and event producers, its existence allows the galera to be more inven-tive and more specialized, taking participants' interests far beyond sexuality or sexual identity and into the uncharted waters of queerness.

Ambivalent Relationship to "Bourgeois" Society

Bohemia has long been understood as oppositional to the "bourgeois" order (Wilson 2000; Lause 2009; Levin 2010). For the galera this is per-haps most evident in its creation of a social world that stands in for the

---

[9] It is not to say that no participants in the galera are concerned with sex and sexual iden-tity. Many are, but the galera and the nocturnal bohemia as a whole are much less so. I take up this discussion in Chap. 6.

more conventional kinds of middle-class sociality offered by Teresina's nightlife. To be a member of the middle class and to opt out of opportunities to perform, maintain, and increase one's social status, is, in some respects, to refuse the dominant social order and its future-oriented temporality (Halberstam 2005). This position also plays out in galera discourse about a pervasive attitude of self-importance and superficiality among members of Teresina's expanding middle class. Still others talk about *"referência"* ("reference") to claim their distinction from mainstream society.

Sérgio, for example, tells me that because so many people in Teresina have an inferiority complex about their city and state and think it is "the asshole of the world," they are impressed by virtually anything from *fora* (places outside Teresina imagined to be superior). "They are very passive. They accept anything," he tells me. Sérgio explains that it is these kinds of people who don't have *"referência."* By *referência*, Sérgio is referring to having a sophisticated understanding of something—particularly a culture, an aesthetic, an event, or a practice—that is imagined to exist in another place or time. For Sérgio, most upwardly mobile Teresinenses desire only that which they perceive to be superior to them and lack a sense of what lies beneath that perceived superiority. According to Sérgio, not having referência is visible in people's superficial appreciation for something; they don't like it for what it *is*, but rather for what it does for their status. Sérgio cited the example of his aunt who, upon returning from a trip to Paris, had little more than clichés to share—for example, photos of the Eiffel Tower and the Arc de Triomphe.

A different but related notion of referência can be seen in an anecdote that a performance artist named Rafael relayed to me. Rafael traveled to the countryside of the neighboring state, Ceará, to a small town to conduct a workshop for a group of amateur contemporary dancers and performance artists. "They wanted me to teach them how to get naked!" he told me with a chuckle (his performance group has developed a somewhat scandalous reputation for occasionally incorporating nudity into its performances). Rafael continued, "They are quite immature. But seriously, it's incredible what referência can do. It can't do it all, but at least they become ready and open to learn how to do new things." Rafael's use of referência is broader than that of Sérgio. For Rafael, referência speaks to the general power embedded in the desire to approximate that which is far away and unfamiliar—the cosmopolitan process of incorporating distant ways of life into one's local existence, whether imagined or practiced.

In Teresina, where these kinds of cosmopolitan appropriations are on the rapid increase (via greater numbers of human interactions and greater access to distant worlds via new technologies and travel) and are often deployed for status and belonging, a number of participants in the galera characterize their community in contradistinction to the upwardly mobile masses along lines of a superior sense of referência—that is, a truer, more genuine, and more intimate relationship to distant worlds and their aesthetics in particular. While Sérgio believes that most people in Teresina "don't have referência," Rafael's sense of referência is that everyone has it. The difference, for Rafael, lies in the extent to which people pursue a more profound understanding of such outside notions. As such, bohemia stands apart from a "bourgeois" or upwardly mobile mainstream social order in terms of quality of taste and expertise.

Yet like other scholars have shown, bohemia has a complex relationship to the bourgeois order to the extent that bohemia can in fact perpetuate it (Lloyd 2006; Levin 2010; Velho 2002). In his study of Wicker Park's "neobohemians," Lloyd finds that "the activities of artists provide benefits to local economies far beyond what can be measured by formal art markets" (2006: 17). In Teresina, the relationship between the galera's nocturnal bohemia and its mainstream society is equally complex, though it takes a different shape from that which Lloyd observed in Wicker Park. Outside nocturnal bohemia, its participants share social spaces with mainstream society (neighborhoods, malls, bars, restaurants, etc.); maintain close ties to their families (most of which are steeped in mainstream lifestyles) through daily encounters if not shared housing; and are employed by and cater to it in the areas of advertising, event planning, architecture, design, journalism, and commerce. In fact, Bruno's Innovation Workshop, whose clients are members of Teresina's upwardly mobile mainstream, gained inspiration from a galera event: Sérgio's monthly bazaar. While the galera's ethos of experimentation and queer approach to gender/sexuality is inextricably bound to a general rejection of the so-called bourgeois lifestyles, the galera is embedded in Teresina's mainstream society, a discussion I take up in greater detail in Chap. 5.

Conclusion

The ethos of queerness that structures the galera's desires, practices, and shapes the very contours of its nocturnal bohemia seems fitting when one considers Teresina's current state of transition—a city thought to be a cultural backwater now experiencing tremendous population growth; a population with greater purchasing power and access to the world than ever before; and a city dominated by a socially conservative middle class struggling to position itself in a shifting terrain of social distinctions. Might not the galera's queerness—fluidity, flexibility, and openness to possibility—both in terms of identity and community in relation to space and time, be the perfect antidote to such a disorienting world in flux?

Participants in the galera are able to establish a sense of belonging with like-minded others without being restricted to a particular identity category, neighborhood of residence, and without risking one's reputation in the eyes of the mainstream. While nocturnal bohemia certainly serves its purpose for its participants to acquire a queer sense of belonging at the margins of mainstream society, what happens when the night ends? How does the galera maintain itself during the day? Is every night "to be continued...?" And how is the galera able to maintain its ethos of queerness and remain integrated? In the two subsequent chapters—one on family, employment, and the power of normative life, and the other on intimate relationships beyond the family—I address how the galera persists beyond the queer space and time of nocturnal bohemia.

References

Allison, Anne. 2001. Cyborg Violence: Bursting Borders and Bodies with Queer Machines. *Cultural Anthropology* 16 (2): 237–265.

Bersani, L. 1996. *Homos*. Cambridge, MA: Harvard University Press.

Brown, Marilyn. 1985. *Gypsies and Other Bohemians: The Myth of the Artist in Nineteenth-Century France*. Ann Arbor: UMI Research Press.

Butler, Judith. 1990. *Gender Trouble: Feminism and the Subversion of Identity*. New York: Routledge.

Chauncey, George. 1994. *Gay New York: Gender, Urban Culture, and the Making of the Gay Male World, 1890–1940*. New York: Basic Books.

Dean, Tim. 2009. *Unlimited Intimacy: Reflections on the Subculture of Barebacking*. Chicago: University of Chicago Press.

Edelman, Lee. 1995. Queer Theory: Unstating Desire. *GLQ* 2: 343–346.

———. 1998. The Future is Kid Stuff: Queer Theory, Disidentification, and the Death Drive. *Narrative* 6: 18–30.

Graña, César, and Marigay Graña. 1990. *On Bohemia: The Code of the Self-Exiled*. New Brunswick: Transaction Publishers.

Halberstam, Judith. 2005. *In a Queer Time and Place: Transgender Bodies, Subcultural Lives*. New York: New York University Press.

Lause, Mark A. 2009. *The Antebellum Crisis & America's First Bohemians*. Kent: Kent State University Press.

Levin, Joanna. 2010. *Bohemia in America, 1858–1920*. Stanford: Stanford University Press.

Lloyd, Richard. 2006. *Neo-Bohemia: Art and Commerce in the Postindustrial City*. New York: Routledge.

McCallum, E.L., and Mikko Tuhkanen. 2011. *Queer Times, Queer Becomings*. Albany: SUNY Press.

Velho, Gilberto. 2002. *A Utopia Urbana: Um Estudo de Antropologia Social*. Rio de Janeiro: Jorge Zahar Editor.

Wilson, Elizabeth. 2000. *Bohemians: The Glamorous Outcasts*. New Brunswick: Rutgers University Press.

CHAPTER 5

Black Sheep by Day

Abstract The chapter brings the reader from nocturnal bohemia back out into the day, exposing Teresina's bohemians in the context of the ordinary and the normal. Rather than transcending mainstream local life, the bohemians find themselves in constant negotiation with it. The chapter addresses how these bohemians negotiate double lives—participating in both the nightlife of bohemia and the "daylife" of mainstream society. Part of this negotiation means deploying different discourses and practices in different spaces and moments. The chapter argues that it is through such negotiations and its ethos of queerness (e.g., fluidity, flexibility, and openness to possibility) that the community of bohemians makes sense of the contradiction of being both local and cosmopolitan.

Keywords Belonging • Cosmopolitanism • Mainstream society • Double-life

"Damn! Teresina wakes up early" I said glancing up at Raquel as I tried to smash the ice into smaller pieces. "Just like in the countryside," she replied.

It was just before seven o'clock in the morning on a Tuesday in July. Raquel had offered to take me on a day trip to her hometown, São Miguel dos Milagres. São Miguel is a little town in the countryside of Piauí, only a few hours' drive from Teresina, at least when the roads are in decent

© The Author(s) 2019   97
T. E. Murphy, *Queerly Cosmopolitan*,
https://doi.org/10.1007/978-3-030-00296-1_5

repair. Raquel's parents were traveling, so she had access to her mom's car. She wanted to be sure to leave early so we would arrive and have a chance to venture around town a bit before the heat set in. Parked at a gas station at the edge of town with the sun coming up in the distance, we did our last-minute preparations: Raquel checked the pressure of the tires, and I readied a hefty blue thermos of soon-to-be cold water.

"You've noticed that Teresina is just like a small town, right?" Raquel asked. "Well sort of, but how do you mean exactly?" I asked. "I mean... I don't know...like the way people act." Raquel continued as I worked to fit the irregularly shaped chunks of ice into the narrow mouth of the thermos.

> People living far from downtown wake up early and ride their bicycles to get downtown to sell the simplest of things—breakfast cakes, coffee, candies, bus tickets, vegetables...you know, all of those things that they sell there at the Old Market and downtown. Sometimes the maid at my parents' house arrives before six o'clock in the morning! Do you believe it? The last time she did, I opened the door and laughed. I said, 'Dona Francisca! Are you crazy? It's a quarter to six in the morning!' She just smiled and said, 'when the sun is rising and people start making noise, I get up. I take a shower, and I go wait for the bus.' Teresina is like a small town at the end of the day too. Haven't you ever noticed how people put chairs in their front doorways at the end of the afternoon and just sit and watch people in the neighborhood? It's no different in the countryside (Fig. 5.1).

As we pulled out of the gas station onto the highway to begin our trip to São Miguel, I tried to imagine what people I know in Teresina were doing around that ripe hour of six-thirty in the morning. Mesmerized by the increasing number of sun-soaked Babaçu, Buriti, and Carnauba palms backdropped by Teresina's strikingly blue sky, my mind shuffled through a number of images: men wearing tattered cowboy hats and loose-fitting shirts that exposed their chests squinting their eyes and pedaling uphill into the sun on rusty Monarch bikes; Lúcio waking up to the stirring of his two cats—Zaha Hadid and Oscar Neimeyer—and then carefully trying to slide into his desk chair to check his Twitter account as his brother sleeps in the trundle bed just next to him; Luana, caressing her spiky-haired head and nearly falling back to sleep as she leans back against her kitchen sink and waits for her coffee water to boil; Dona Luzia, in spandex shorts, flip-flops and an old t-shirt, temporarily abandoning her busy stove of couscous, tapioca, and sweet coffee to chase after Marcelinho and

Fig. 5.1   Leaving Teresina

keep him from bothering his mother as she readies herself for work; João waking up to the sounds of Axê music pouring out of the gym across the street from his ten-story condominium; Anderson, still asleep in his hammock, automatically turning off his air conditioner with a flick of his big toe and then wrapping himself tighter in a sheet; Jaír, hot, exhausted, and irritated, waking to Isabel nudging him to get up and feed six-month-old Paulinho; Claudia lathering her hair in cream and envisioning herself happily employed as she prepares for her eight o'clock interview at the Parnaíba department store; Walter throwing on a pair of brightly colored shorts and grabbing his towel from the line as he saunters out back in his flip-flops for his morning shower, thinking about how he will manage to fix his flat tire before biking over to rehearsal.

"You have no idea." Raquel grinned, glancing over at me. "The people in São Miguel are going to lose it when they see this gringo! They won't know what to do with you!" she cackled. Raquel would know. She spent most of her childhood there, until age 13 when her parents relocated the

family to Teresina so that she and her brothers could receive a better education than what was available in São Miguel. Raquel began to recall her
childhood.

> Back there, we didn't have Internet or cell phones, and there were probably
> only four or five houses in the whole town that had a telephone at all—we
> were one of them. There were probably ten or fifteen houses with people
> who had some money and the rest were poor. It was like the "countryside
> of the countryside." People had nothing. Nowadays, people have more.
> Before, all the houses were made of straw—walls and roof. They were so
> poor they couldn't even make houses of clay...much less brick. Because
> straw comes from nature, they would just rip straw from the ground and
> make a house. There was no electricity. I would go with my mom to visit her
> hometown and there, all the houses had little straw outhouses. We would
> take the water from the well to take a bath. I had lots of contact with this
> kind of way of life. It was only later that I had contact with other things...
> other foods. At my house, we always ate regional foods. Only when we came
> to Teresina did I try things like yogurt and pizza. We didn't have very many
> industrialized things. My dad would come to Teresina much more than the
> rest of us, and sometimes he would bring things back. At that time, the road
> was mostly dirt. When I moved to Teresina, it was a huge shock. All the
> people, different kinds of people...it was crazy.

Raquel's story is not unlike that of a number of participants in the galera[1]
who also grew up in the country and later moved to Teresina. Her description reminded me of Gustavo, a galera participant in his early 40s who
once told me about his experience growing up in a little town called Padre
Carvalho, also in the countryside of Piauí (Figs. 5.2 and 5.3).

> It's pretty typical for a small Northeastern town: little thirteen year-old
> boys ride motorcycles; everyone drinks; you can imagine. In Padre
> Carvalho, I was a princess, a little girl...very delicate...with a delicate voice.
> My dad was a teacher. I was pointed at a lot—one of the *bichinhas* (little
> gay boys) in town. I used to get beat up. My mom's family had a farm on
> the outskirts of town...I remember walking with my mom one time out
> there near the farm. I didn't have a shirt on. We came upon this woman
> who said, "I didn't know you had such a big daughter." My mom said,

---

[1] The "galera" refers to the clique of people who come together to form Teresina's nocturnal bohemia (Chap. 4).

Fig. 5.2 Countryside town, late morning

Fig. 5.3 Countryside town, late morning

"He's my son." That made me really sad. My mom and I were super close when I was young. I cried like crazy when I came here to Teresina. She wanted me to move here to study high school and English. She couldn't do it when she was young, so she wanted me to. I'm the oldest, so she sent me first. When I arrived, I was only twelve years old. I only had clothes that were made by my aunt. She was a great seamstress. But still, nothing of mine was bought in a store. I remember the first shirt that I bought. I saw it on a novela. It was so important to me—it made me feel OK in society. Back in Padre Carvalho I was in my own little world. When I came here, I wanted to know all about this new world—books, fashion, etc. What saved me is that I liked to study, and I got good grades. At sixteen, I started college. But soon after I started studying I knew I didn't want to be an accountant. I wanted to know the world.

About half way to São Miguel, we turned off onto a cracked asphalt road full of potholes, and our speed was cut in half. Raquel told me this was normal. She also explained that this was far from the worst of scenarios. She said that there was a possibility that we would get to a point where we wouldn't even be able to make it to São Miguel. Sometimes seasonal rains erode segments of the road so much that it becomes impossible to make the journey in a small car.

Other participants in the galera have similar connections to countryside towns. Like Gustavo, a number of men and women in the galera were sent to Teresina during their adolescence to attend school and live with relatives, in student homes, or in apartments some distance from downtown and the East Zone with a maid to watch over them. Because their parents and younger siblings remained back at home in the countryside, many participants would regularly return home on holidays to spend time with friends and family. Once they grew older, most began to return home less often, but like other participants who were born and raised in Teresina, they travel to the countryside for special occasions like relatives' birthdays, Easter, and other holidays.

Once Raquel and I finally arrived to São Miguel, we had to circumvent a massive mud puddle at the town's entrance. Raquel proceeded along a dirt road that ran along the edge of town. She said she first wanted to show me where her grandparents' land was. After seeing it, we passed by a small bar where five young men with short hair wearing shorts, tank tops, and flip-flops were sitting and looking out on to the road. As we passed by them, they stared at us in bewilderment. Raquel, behind the wheel with her short pink and brown curly hair, me, riding shotgun with long shaggy hair and a beard, and the two of us wearing large plastic sunglasses, perhaps seemed a bit out of place. When we smiled back at them, all five suddenly burst into laughter, causing us to laugh just as hard. Raquel turned to me and quipped, "Didn't I tell you?!"

As we toured around the town, passing the Catholic Church, the school, and the house where Raquel grew up, I noticed that perhaps it wasn't only our unconventional appearances that caused people to stare. There was very little movement on the streets in general, and we were but one of a handful of cars and motorcycles in sight. Of the few men and women that we did see on the street, most were either on foot or riding bicycles. Within no more than 10 or 15 minutes, Raquel turned to me and said, "Well, that's São Miguel. It's really small and simple, hua?"

Over time, I would eventually discover that while not all my friends in the galera are *from* São Miguel, they all know São Miguel. Quite well as a matter of fact. Maybe not the São Miguel I visited with Raquel, but *other* São Miguels scattered about the state of Piauí.

CEZANNE'S GAS STATION

"You guys!! That idiot almost ran over that girl!" Raquel exclaimed, throwing her arms in the air after we watched a new silver Toyota sedan tear down the road and then screeching its tires, whip into the gas station and nearly clip a girl walking to her car.

It was around three in the morning. Some friends and I had been hanging out across the street from the gas station for an hour or so on the steps of a recently built mini strip mall yet to be occupied. A few hours earlier, we had been dancing to Sérgio's indie-rock set that he carefully selected for the second of Raquel's new monthly party, hosted at our friend Fabio's punk bar that he transformed out of an abandoned house. It had proven to be yet another success, bringing in a little over 100 people. After packing up Raquel's mom's hatchback with the sound equipment, Raquel suggested that we head over to Cezanne's, the new all-hours gas station for one more beer. With bars now closing by 2 am due to the new curfew ordinance, a select few gas stations selling alcohol on the sly were our only hope for keeping the party going. We were sitting across the street from the gas station on the curb of a nearly completed strip mall when we witnessed the man in the Toyota nearly hit the woman walking.

"No kidding, you guys. I hate that. A daddy's-boy who takes his father's new car just to drive around and act like a jerk. I hate it!" said Paulo, leaning against the wall in his tight hotpink pants and flipping his long bangs out of his face as he puffed on a cigarette.

"Where are guys like that from? Here in the East Zone?" I asked. "Probably, but who knows," Raquel said as she looked up from rolling a joint.

> Nowadays they could be from practically any part of town—the East Zone, the South Zone, even Mocambinho.[2] Have you ever noticed how all of the "*chique*" (chic) bars and clubs here in the East Zone are all pretty close to one another? Well these *mafrenses* just come here to show off, driving up and down the same streets in their daddy's cars, wasted drunk, acting like jerks.

MAFRENSE CHIQUE

That was not the first time I heard my friends in the galera distinguish themselves from the so-called *mafrenses* and their attempts to be seen as chique. Mafrense is an in-group term that some of my friends have appropriated. Mafrense is said to be the surname of one of the first Portuguese families to settle the state of Piauí. Over time it became a category that some people claiming to be "truly Teresinense" would use to distinguish themselves from newcomers. The galera's appropriation of the name, however, has given it a new connotation. For many in the galera, mafrense points to people attempting to appear chique while maintaining a lifestyle and outlook that is stereotypically local and parochial, ranging from small-minded and naive to close-minded, ignorant, and inconsiderate. Many in the galera consider the very idea of chique to be flawed. For them, chique is inherently superficial, an artifice, a performance that tries to mask an authentic self. As such, they are critical of the very project of appropriating goods, services, and practices solely for their so-called chique-ness in the attempt to convince/deceive others.

Though the galera deploys "mafrense" and "chique," and related terms in a variety of ways, most often its members invoke them to point to Teresinenses who are engaged in uncouth and self-important performances of chique; ridiculing a young man for driving his fathers' new car

---

[2] Mocambinho began as a government-subsidized housing development (*conjunto habitacional*) and has since grown, become quite established, and is now home to a number of Teresina's upwardly mobile residents.

recklessly to show off is just one example. Through the use of mafrense, my friends are able to express their disapproval of the kinds of attitudes, politics, and behaviors that Teresinenses of all social strata sometimes demonstrate in their attempts to be seen as chique: ignorance and machismo; greed for money and power; an attitude of self-importance that results in impoliteness, laziness, and superficiality; and a general disregard for ethics, culture, and education. That said, I have heard each of my friends express that not all mafrenses are bad, and that, in fact, there are a good number of mafrenses they like. Many mafrenses, they say, are simply naive, conservative, and desiring of recognition. Nevertheless, calling people "mafrense" helps the galera reaffirm that it is distinct from a growing class of people that often embody a politics that the galera considers less than ideal.

If the previous chapter examined how the galera manifests as a bohemia at night, this chapter brings the galera back out into the bright daylight of Teresina, exposing its bohemians in the context of the quotidian, the ordinary, and the normal. To demonstrate how the galera sees itself as inextricably bound to Teresina's normative society, this chapter examines bohemians' relationships to everyday life, employment, and the family. No matter how much one's imagination is structured by distant worlds, the material reality of where one resides always matters. As participants in the galera pursue daily needs, wants, and obligations in Teresina, they are often reminded of the extent to which they are indeed part and parcel of the "local."[3]

Nocturnal Bohemians as Local Cosmopolitans

At times, and especially through its nocturnal bohemia (see Chap. 4), the galera creates an existence that looks and feels starkly different from mainstream life in Teresina. The galera's unconventional taste in aesthetics, its alternative politics, and its beliefs in social equality more generally sometimes make the world the galera forges feel entirely foreign to the kind of life one regularly encounters in Teresina. A well-traveled performance artist visiting from Rio de Janeiro remarked to me one evening at a galera

[3] It is important to note that neither does the galera nor do I take the "local" to be anything more than a relative, context-contingent, or "conjured" (Tsing 2005: 57) geographical scale.

event, "If I didn't know better, I swear to you, I would think that I was at an underground party in Berlin!" Yet in other moments, it is almost impossible to ignore the extent to which the galera is deeply embedded in Teresinense life. During fieldwork, it became apparent that resisting temptations that tend to ground participants in local life, such as worrying about other people's business, trying to measure up to others' expectations, and conforming to social conventions, can often prove quite challenging. It is as if *fora* (places far from Teresina imagined to be superior) and the infinite possibility of different ways of life that underpin the galera's ethos and practices become obscured by life "on the ground."

This experience of belonging at once to one's immediate surroundings and distant worlds makes it possible to understand the galera as a community of local cosmopolitans. Though cosmopolitans were once thought to be synonymous with world travelers (Robbins 1998; Rapport and Stade 2007) and sophisticated metropolises (Calhoun 2008), recent scholarship in the social sciences has begun to consider the power of the cosmopolitan imagination (Meskimmon 2011; Delanty 2009) and the formation of locally "rooted" cosmopolitan subjectivities (Appiah 1998; Breckenridge et al. 2002). These bodies of social science literature demonstrate how global flows and the imagination can lead people to understand themselves as at once "local" and "cosmopolitan" (Novak 2010; Scheld 2007). Though the galera thrives on much that is unconventional, fora-inspired, and uncommon to Teresina—interests that structure a shared ethos of imagined belonging on both national (Anderson 1983) and supranational (Appadurai 1996) scales—its daily existence is deeply entrenched in local life.

With nocturnal bohemia structuring much of the galera's sociality, the galera can be seen, also, as both cosmopolitan and bohemian—an intersection of orientations that is not altogether uncommon (e.g. Lause 2009; Velho 2002). Bohemia that developed after that of mid-nineteenth-century Montparnasse, Paris, in places like New York and London were, according to Lause, "innately cosmopolitan and internationalist" (Lause 2009: viii). In his book, *The Antebellum Crisis and America's First Bohemians*, Lause writes about an American abolitionist named Henry Clapp Jr. Elaborating on Clapp, Lause writes, "He became a cosmopolite not just by his own choice but by choosing to experience that choice overseas. While there, he encountered, admired, and, again by choice, assimilated the values of bohemian Paris and London" (Lause 2009: 2). Upon returning to New York, Clapp participated in what he referred to as a "complicated secret institution" (Lause 2009: 21) comprised of men and women who were "open to the experience of new worlds, and this includes some of the earliest Orientalists in the United States and some pioneers in the recreational uses of psychoactive substances" (Lause 2009: 2). As the bohemian sentiment traveled, it began to develop an imagined cosmopolitan community of bohemians, who, like the galera, would come to understand their alternative stance toward mainstream society and engagement in unconventional practices as indivisible from other like-minded peoples and places throughout the world.

Still, the galera largely differs from bohemia of the mid-nineteenth century. Something of a refuge from quotidian pressures to conform to social norms and to be seen as chique, nocturnal bohemia temporarily disintegrates with the dawn of each new day and the galera is faced with the limits of its underground cosmopolitan-bohemian world. And though participants carry their queer sensibilities with them throughout the day, the local, material existence of Teresina has a cunning power to root, embed, and ground the galera in its mainstream society.

INEVITABLE AS DAY

If Teresina's sweltering heat, large lower class, and "rurban" landscape ever fail to remind those in the galera of exactly where it is that they reside, staring strangers are sure to bring them home. Many Teresinenses are attentive to difference and accustomed to staring. Whether riding on buses, walking on streets, exiting cars in front of restaurants, walking through the mall, waiting at a stoplight, or sitting at a bar, locals often can be found scrutinizing and talking about strangers or even just staring at them apathetically or with bafflement. Why so many Teresinenses are accustomed to staring is not a simple question to answer. While I have a few hunches, they are in no way complete or conclusive. However, one particular point seems significant: recent rural-urban migration from the countryside makes for a widespread fascination with difference, whether due to how novel, chique, or strange a person may appear. Since the mid-twentieth century, in much of Brazil—of which Teresina is a case in point—rural-urban migration has increased at unprecedented rates. Thus, people from small towns who are not accustomed to as much variety as one tends to find among larger populations may be more likely to find themselves transfixed on the apparent differences of other residents. The scene at the start of this chapter where the young men in São Miguel stared and laughed at Raquel and me is an example of this tendency. Especially for Teresina's upwardly mobile masses, these stares have the power to "normalize" (Foucault 1995: 184) residents, prompting them to police their appearances and practices so that they conform to the conventional. For participants in the galera, who often wear unconventional clothing, hairstyles, and accouterments, these stares not only serve as a reminder of just how normative their city is; they have an additional effect: they remind participants that they are indeed different, if not foreign, in Teresina. While participants may find such stares irritating at times, such attention does little to normalize participants' appearances and actions. If anything, these stares only reinforce participants' cosmopolitan subjectivity and sense of belonging in the galera. Thus, stares simultaneously localize the galera and give it flight back to the cosmopolitan world to which it be-longs.

Receiving stares is not all that roots the galera in local life. In pursuing everyday activities, participants confront limitations and shortcomings typical to Brazil and the Northeast, further embedding them in daily life and its seeming inevitability. Participants occasionally bemoan that there is nothing to do in Teresina; that it is too hot to go for a walk during the day and too dangerous to go for a stroll at night. Other times, they express frustration about the conditions of public and private education; about how much better local art, design, and architecture could be; about how the city's bus system ought to function; about how much more diverse the city could be in terms of employment and industry; about how locals with money don't know how to invest wisely in their city; about locals' selfishness and lack of concern for one another; and about the recurrent problems with corruption in all forms of government. On these fronts and others, participants in the galera sometimes feel helpless and somewhat cynical about their ability to improve such conditions. Yet participants do not cease to care about their city; they dream of how it could be better and different, and nocturnal bohemia is one way they attempt to realize such dreams. Nevertheless, with continual reminders of their city, state, and nation's shortcomings and the far reach of long-established power structures, the "local" becomes something that can feel not only palpable but also inescapable.

In other moments, when participants take part in pastimes that they see as somewhat unique to their city, region, or nation they are confronted by their attachments to Teresina in a more positive light. While sharing a bottle of the "coldest beer in Brazil" at a long-standing watering hole in downtown, Isabel and Vitor might lovingly joke about how people in the countryside talk. While passing through his old neighborhood on the way to the Piçarra Market to join local drag queens and travestis to eat a traditional soup or tapioca cakes after a long night out, Igor might reminisce about his youth with friends. On a late afternoon, Raquel and Maria might venture out to the meeting of the city's two rivers to relax, eat popsicles made of local fruits, and listen to a child from the neighborhood recount a local legend for some spare change. After a full week of teaching art classes, Ruth might spend several hours preparing her costume for a Carnival parade while André and Cássia enthusiastically plan a trip to the countryside to visit a waterfall or go hunting for amethyst or opal. And not so seldom will various participants in the galera remark about just how unique their galera is—asserting that in the greater context of Brazil and the world, its particular combination of tastes in music, its specific access to resources for producing events, and its particular mixture of different kinds of people and attitudes creates a community that is like no other.

What most often roots the galera in local-ness, however, are practices that are so usual that participants rarely recognize them—practices that Robert Rotenberg (1995) might attribute to "metropolitan knowledge." To be a local in Teresina is to know how to navigate the city; to know where and when traffic becomes dense; to know where and when it is legal to disregard a red light to avoid an armed assault; to know how to deal with streets where left turns are forbidden; to know where not to speed due to bumps and potholes that could otherwise ruin one's car; to know how to avoid police checkpoints; to know when the sun is at its hottest and to know how to avoid it; to know a variety of local remedies for dehydration; to know how to cope with an insect called Potó, which is unique to the area and can burn and scar the skin; to know which streets flood during a January downpour and how to get around them; to know all sorts of conventions around status symbols tied to gender, "race," class, age, and marital status; to know when to code switch and how to put on appropriate airs for particular settings; to know the gossip about important local people; and to know who to talk to in order to resolve problems that range from those related to the law, to interior design, to producing an event.

The material conditions of everyday life in Teresina, from those that participants critique, to those that they praise, ground their cosmopolitan sense of belonging in the local. As Sarah Green writes in her ethnography

Notes from the Balkans: Locating Marginality and Ambiguity on the Greek-Albanian Border, "being where you are and being from somewhere always matters, even if it does not mean you stay in one place, either physically or perceptually, for any length of time" (2005: 1). Whether one finds belonging in imagined communities (Anderson 1983) or global "scapes" (Appadurai 1996), the so-called global and cosmopolitan identifications are always localized in place (Boellstorff 2005; Donham 1998; Condry 2001; Scheld 2007). That said, what distinguishes local cosmopolitans in one location from another are not only different appropriations of the global but also the local mechanisms that root such cosmopolitan orientations. For the galera, in the context of Teresina, two of the most prominent localizing mechanisms are families and clients.

FAMILY

The institution of the family is central to daily life in the Brazilian Northeast. One of the chief reproducers of social norms and habitus (Bourdieu 1984), the family bears a significant influence on the galera. While the trend seems to be changing slowly, with few exceptions participants in the galera of all ages live with their parents or in property owned by a family member. Like many Brazilians, a number of these men and women also receive familial assistance throughout the course of their lives (Carlo et al. 2007) in obtaining a private education, gainful employment, and the opportunity to enjoy travel and other leisure activities. As a result, familial support reinforces participants' roles as daughters, sons, sisters, brothers, granddaughters, grandsons, nieces, and nephews. Although the galera's relationship to the family might be characterized as typically Brazilian, it is still rather unique. Throughout Brazil, as in much of the world, it is often the case that one's family bears a significant influence on one's social position and reputation (Bourdieu 1984), and Teresina is no exception. Overwhelmingly, to be without a family (and perhaps more importantly a family name) is, at best, to be unimportant; at worst, it is to be a social outcast. Yet the family has an added significance in a city like Teresina. As an inland and comparatively new and underdeveloped capital of one of Brazil's poorest states, Teresina offers a limited set of employment opportunities for a single person to be able to afford an apartment and maintain the middle-class lifestyle that many participants in the galera are accustomed to enjoying. Unlike wealthier, more industrialized cities in Brazil, where job markets are more diverse, professions in law, medicine, and public service are the safest routes to ensuring a sustainable middle-class lifestyle in Teresina. Often embedded in local familial networks, these and other forms of employment prove yet another reason to maintain close relationships with one's family.

While the galera's ethos of queerness often corresponds with participants feeling like outsiders in relation to mainstream society, a similar experience can occur within the family. A fair number of daughters and sons are considered the black sheep (*ovelhas negras*) of their families, often refusing to conform to lifestyles thought to be appropriate for their gender and/or social standing. Often, black sheep long to leave Teresina and start a life elsewhere, yet are discouraged by their families' wishes for them to remain close. Other black sheep become convinced that maintaining the quality of life that they enjoy in Teresina is untenable elsewhere and, thus, fear failure in an attempt to leave home. Black sheep are also closely tied to their families because most of them do not pursue heteronormative lifestyles—that is, many are not sexually or romantically involved with members of the opposite sex and, thus, do not expect to have families of their own. Consequently, despite their black sheep role, many sons and daughters remain in close physical and often emotional proximity to their parents, siblings, and other relatives.

Although living with and/or being financially dependent on one's family may afford individual participants a particular middle-class lifestyle, this arrangement can present a number of challenges, many of which the galera—seen as a cosmopolitan project—strives to overcome. The galera sets up boundaries between itself and mainstream society to carve out a distinct community for its participants. Nocturnal bohemia is one obvious way that the galera distinguishes itself from mainstream society, but the rhetorical devices of *mafrense*, *chique*, and *referência* that participants use are other ways of establishing boundaries. Earlier in this chapter, for example, I show how mafrense and chique both serve the galera to position itself as separate from residents who attempt to appear superior to, and sometimes at the expense of, other locals. As a result, the galera becomes something other than stereotypically local and parochial, actively rejecting dominant prejudices around "race," class, and gender/sexuality. Additionally, as I show in Chap. 4, having *referência*—a profound understanding of distant worlds and their aesthetics and lifeways—also distinguishes the galera from the upwardly mobile masses, helping it see itself as something authentic rather than a superficial and status-motivated investment in fora. Referência allows the galera to conceive of itself as genuinely invested in distant worlds and lifeways in establishing a sense of belonging to the world rather than in the "little world" of Teresina. Thus, in the sense that the galera's bohemian-cosmopolitanism is something of a project intended to carve out a queer space of belonging in Teresina, it is often undermined by participants' families' position within, and/or ties to, mainstream society. Thus, while the family's economic support enables the galera's existence and survival, the family also contributes to its inability to fully realize its bohemian and cosmopolitan ideals.

On numerous fronts, the family challenges the galera's cosmopolitan ideals. One example is being open and receptive to difference. Deeply rooted in a local habitus of mistrust (Ansell 2008),[4] some families show profound skepticism of others. Before going to my friend Gabriella's house for the first time, she warned me that her parents are rather aloof. I asked her to explain what she meant.

> They're just not very open with people they don't know. When a stranger comes to their house, they don't know if the person is there to do harm or not. It's just the way people from the countryside are. They are always mistrustful.

Gabriella, nearly 40 years old, lives with her grandparents in a medium-sized, two-bedroom home with a maid's quarters on the periphery of the East Zone, only one block away from her parent's house. Though participating in the galera feeds Gabriella's curiosity and desire to approximate the unfamiliar, she is aware that sometimes her parents' aloofness influences her ability to be receptive to unfamiliar people she encounters at galera events.

Participants' parents' conventional attitudes about gender roles also can be difficult to resist despite the galera's ethos of queerness and ideal of gender equality. Ricardo's parents are both from countryside of Piauí and relocated to Teresina about 15 years ago to work in the public sector when Ricardo was only 12. They live in a relatively small three-bedroom apartment in the East Zone and share one car. Ricardo, who is openly gay, has

---

[4] Aaron Ansell, in his article "'But the winds will turn against you': An analysis of wealth forms and the discursive space of development in northeast Brazil," concludes that in the community he studied in the south of Piauí, locals fear telling others about wealth in terms of land and livestock that is subject to danger by the Evil Eye. While Ansell's focus is community development, his findings reveal a tendency one can find throughout the countryside of Piauí: a habitus of mistrust of others.

a contentious relationship with his family that he attributes to his sexual orientation. Although in the past his parents were more overt in their disapproval of his lifestyle, today they simply refuse to acknowledge it. While Ricardo's gay identity is no secret to the galera, he admits that *machista* (machismo) culture (e.g., Guttman 1996), which is especially pronounced in the Northeast (De Albuquerque Junior 2003) and engrained in Ricardo's family's values, has influenced his prejudice toward men who he thinks act too effeminate or go too far experimenting with their gender.

Overt expressions of classism, which are not uncommon throughout Brazil, are another rooting mechanism. Despite the galera's ideals of social equality, attitudes expressed by participants' families that challenge such ideals can prove quite difficult to shirk. A few participants, for example, grew up in households with *"filhos de criação,"* meaning informally adopted children from very poor families who are sent by their parents to work in homes as domestic servants in exchange for room, board, and schooling. Looking back on their childhoods, these participants sometimes have difficulty not blaming the "filhos" themselves for their eventual estrangement from the host family and lack of economic success later in life. Despite the fact that filhos de criação are never treated as full members of the family, participants sometimes allude to filhos' outcomes as a result of their essential difference rather than their circumstances. Other relatively socially acceptable classist practices learned from families that occasionally creep into participants' daily conversations are: referencing aesthetics that they dislike as *"pobre"* ("poor"); deriding participants in the galera who come from less economically established families in ways that speak to their lower economic status; and criticizing the decision to become a full-time artist in Teresina due to its association with poverty.

Like the family, mainstream conventions and limited opportunities for employment and leisure can often feel unavoidable, yet the opposite is also sometimes true—the galera's close relationship to the family can enable and even encourage its ethos of cosmopolitanism and queerness. The economic support families provide affords the galera time—time to surf the Internet, time to blog, time to tweet, time to conjure up plans for new events, time to chat with friends across the city on Instant Messenger, time to listen to and learn about new music, time to travel, and time to take part in nocturnal bohemia. In short, the family provides the time necessary for the galera to exist. Additionally, a number of families have stimulated their children's openness to different cultures and difference by saving up to send them to Jesuit and other private schools in which a "cultural education" is privileged over a career-oriented one. Some participants also refer to their family's more direct cultivation of their unconventional interests: as sons and daughters of local artists and actors, a select few are second-generation participants in the galera; others have parents who enrolled them in art classes and allowed them to pursue artistic projects such as painting, sculpture, dance, music, and theater; and many families encouraged their children at an early age to learn foreign languages and maintain contacts with pen pals in distant countries. It bears noting that not all participants face the same amount of pressure to conform to social norms, albeit for different reasons, which may influence their parents' reactions to their children's unconventional tastes. For example, some families toward the lower end of the middle-class spectrum depend on their black sheeps' contributions to the family household income and, thus, are often less critical of their alternative interests and lifestyles.

Far more than a collection of individuals, places like Teresina are made up of families, and familial networks are the social fabric through which daily life takes shape. Though families may be at least partly responsible for the galera's sense that everyday life in Teresina is predictable, oppressive, and inescapable, some families in particular are equally responsible for the galera's ideals of social equality and desires to challenge convention, to dream of new possibilities, and to conjure up novel projects and events for their city.

EMPLOYMENT

Inextricably bound to the institution of the family, career opportunities prove equally powerful in their ability to root the galera in local life and bear an influence on its cosmopolitan orientation to the world. The majority of participants in the galera who pursue artistic careers (architecture, design, dance, event production, and advertising) and otherwise (small businesses, foreign language education, retail, journalism, law, and public service) cater to and are employed by Teresinenses who are firmly rooted in its mainstream society. Like individual families, such clients and employers wield a grounding influence over the galera.

To launch their Innovation Workshop, Bruno and his colleagues hosted a cocktail party at the home of one of their relatives who had an elaborately landscaped backyard in a recently built neighborhood in the East Zone. Invested in impressing potential clients and getting the word out about their advertising agency, they invited only a select few participants in the galera who are well known for their established careers as designers and event producers. I arrived with Eduardo and Sérgio, both of whom are accustomed to attending and producing such events. Bruno greeted us just after entering the gate and promptly told us that they were still getting set up but that we could help ourselves to some finger foods and drinks if we liked. He immediately felt the need to explain that there would be no alcohol served—he and his colleagues had decided that not serving alcohol would be essential if they were to ensure that the evening would run smoothly and they would have a chance at impressing future clients.

The three of us sat at a table beneath some banana trees chatting about the setup of the cocktail party and about producing events in Teresina more generally. I had met Eduardo several times before, but this was the first time I had the opportunity to speak with him about his work. Though he majored in accounting in college, Eduardo has been in the business of producing important events in Teresina ever since graduating. For roughly the past 30 years, he has produced a wide range of events from receptions for political parties and business openings, to large-scale music concerts, weddings, graduations, high-end *festas* (parties), and lavish birthday parties. Because Sérgio also occasionally produces these kinds of events, the cocktail party proved an ideal setting for me to learn about their work.

With light lounge music playing in the background, Eduardo turned to me and said, "You've probably noticed that people here like novelty, right?" He continued to explain that the only problem is that many Teresinenses with money think they like innovation but quickly discover that they are not as receptive to trying out new things as they would like to think. He and Sérgio had been discussing this problem just the night before about a wedding they were both contracted to orchestrate. The bride wanted a "super modern" wedding and reception with not even one flower involved in the décor. Yet with only one week prior to the wedding, she had come to Sérgio with an emergency: she wanted flowers. Her family and friends had convinced her that a wedding isn't a wedding without flowers and that if she still refused, they would take it upon themselves to procure them. To avoid disaster, she decided to consult her planners.

While Sérgio was telling his story, more guests began to arrive, and the cocktail party began to take shape: a red runway carpet had been rolled out, a projector began running images of a few different local designers' logos on a large white Lycra screen, the deejay was in place, and a local television reporter began interviewing the founders of the Innovation Workshop. The majority of the guests were women of various ages wearing medium-length, form-fitting skirts or dresses and high heels, with long, straight(ened) hair. I asked Eduardo who they were. He explained that they were all surely from the East Zone and were likely the children, cousins, or friends of some of their clients. Within minutes, a couple of such women approached our table to greet Sérgio and Eduardo and engage in small talk—an occurrence that would happen numerous times throughout the evening. Once the event was over, we made arrangements with Bruno and a few other friends to meet up later at a bar.

In the car, I was able to speak with Eduardo and Sérgio a bit more candidly about the pros and cons of working for clients from traditional and upwardly mobile families in the East Zone. They explained some of the challenges: occasionally producing an event that turns out a bit cheesy (*cafona*) or overly ostentatious; working for clients who, though respected, have reputations for corruption and/or exploiting their workers; having to maintain a relatively tame reputation as a cultural avant-garde and remain tight-lipped about one's grievances with injustices and local politics in order to retain clients; and being expected to support, attend, and speak highly about numerous social events and artistic productions regardless of their quality. Conversations with other participants in the galera over the course of fieldwork revealed additional disadvantages of working with such clients: having to conform to gender norms (including but not limited to concealing one's sexual orientation); often not getting paid on time and/or discovering that one's pay comes from illegitimate sources; and producing expensive and exclusive events that reproduce status and economic hierarchies (Figs. 5.4 and 5.5).

Much like the galera's close ties to family, participants' clients often reinforce normative attitudes and practices, serving to root the galera further in local life. Yet, also like the family, clients can afford participants the chance to realize their aesthetic tastes, and obtain recognition, reinforcing their cosmopolitan subjectivity and sometimes elevating their social status. Though the disadvantages of working for these clients are plenty, Eduardo and Sérgio, as well as other participants, mention numerous advantages to working in cultural production in Teresina, such as: being able to make a name for oneself with one's culturally avant-garde productions—an achievement almost unimaginable in a city of steep competition like São Paulo; being part of a relatively small network of cultural producers and clients through which one is able to develop new skills (e.g., deejaying, producing events, and designing clothing and sets for performances); gaining new job opportunities; starting one's own business; having access

Fig. 5.4 Inside the office of one participant in the galera who makes a living as an architect and a designer

to a wealth of inexpensive materials and labor in producing works of art, textiles, and events; and being able to see one's products on prominent display in the city and in local media.

Though the Innovation Workshop eventually dissolved due to disagreements among its founders, they, as well as other individuals in the galera, have gone on to be quite successful in avant-garde cultural production in Teresina. Igor, who began producing original sculptures and paintings for private residences and high-end businesses, went on to design clothing and open his own high-end boutique in the East Zone selling custom-made

Fig. 5.5 Window display for the business of one participant in the galera who makes a living as a self-taught designer of high-end eveningwear

evening gowns and wedding dresses. Marina, a ballerina, and João, a graphic artist, who began selling trendy t-shirts purchased in São Paulo to friends and family, eventually opened up their own store in the East Zone, selling hip clothing and kitsch novelties. And Alexandre, who studied architecture, has gone on to design everything from new bars and motel renovation projects to large music concerts and sets for local television programs.

CONCLUSION

The galera poses a direct challenge to the inevitability of the ordinary and the normal in Teresina. If the queer world of its nocturnal bohemia were all there was to the galera, one might even be tempted to depict it as having managed to transcend the historical conditions of materiality. Yet, as I have demonstrated in this chapter, such a characterization of the galera would be less than adequate. The galera is part and parcel of the local, and, rather than transcending it, participants in the galera find themselves in constant negotiation with it.

Teresina's normative daily life and the galera are equally dependent on one another. They are mutually constitutive, creating and shaping one another. Normative society, like most systems of oppression, provides opportunities to conjure up alternative frameworks for seeing and being in the world. In this sense, the galera's cosmopolitan ethos is indivisible from the city's rigid, mainstream social structure. The two also mutually constitute one another in more material terms. While mainstream society enables the galera's existence economically via families and clients, the galera can be seen to sustain mainstream status hierarchies in creating and producing avant-garde culture for their clients. Because of this close relationship of dependency, being part of the galera requires continually negotiating belonging on multiple registers—world, nation, region, city, bohemia, work, and family—all of which speak to nuanced perceptions of "local" and "non-local" ways of life. It is through such negotiations that the galera makes sense of the contradiction that one is at once local and global, both inside and outside. Negotiating such contradictions is much of what it means to be a local cosmopolitan in a place like Teresina.

REFERENCES

Anderson, Benedict. 1983. *Imagined Communities: Reflections on the Origin and Spread of Nationalism*. London/New York: Verso.

Ansell, Aaron. 2008. 'But the Winds Will Turn Against You': An Analysis of Wealth-Forms and the Discursive Space of Development in Northeast Brazil. *American Ethnologist* 36 (1): 96–109.

Appadurai, Arjun. 1996. *Modernity at Large: Cultural Dimensions of Globalization*. Minneapolis: University of Minnesota Press.

Appiah, Kwame Anthony. 1998. Cosmopolitan Patriots. In *Cosmopolitics: Thinking and Feeling Beyond the Nation*, ed. Pheng Cheah and Bruce Robbins, 91–114. Minneapolis: University of Minnesota Press.

Boellstorff, Tom. 2005. *The Gay Archipelago: Sexuality and Nation in Indonesia*. Princeton: Princeton University Press.

Bourdieu, Pierre. 1984. *Distinction: A Social Critique of the Judgment of Taste*, Trans. Richard Nice. Cambridge: Harvard University Press.

Breckenridge, Carol A., Sheldon Pollock, Homi K. Bhabha, and Dipesh Chakrabarty, eds. 2002. *Cosmopolitanism*. Durham: Duke University Press.

Calhoun, Craig. 2008. Cosmopolitanism and Nationalism. *Nations and Nationalism* 14 (3): 427–448.

Carlo, Gustavo, Silvia Koller, Marcela Raffaelli, and Maria Rosario de Guzman. 2007. Culture-Related Strengths Among Latin American Families: A Case Study of Brazil. *Faculty Publications, Department of Child, Youth, and Family Studies* 64: 335–360.

Condry, Ian. 2001. Japanese Hip-Hop and the Globalization of Popular Culture. In *Urban Life: Readings in the Anthropology of the City*, ed. George Gmelch and Walter Zenner. Prospect Heights: Waveland Press.

De Albuquerque, Júnior, and Durval Muniz. 2003. *Nordestino: Uma Invenção do Falo: Uma História do Gênero Masculino (Nordeste-1920/1940)*. Maceió: Editora Catavento.

Delanty, Gerard. 2009. *The Cosmopolitan Imagination: The Renewal of Critical Social Theory*. New York: Cambridge University Press.

Donham, Donald. 1998. Freeing South Africa: The "Modernization" of Male-Male Sexuality in Soweto. *Cultural Anthropology* 13 (1): 1–19.

Foucault, Michel. 1995 [1977]. *Discipline and Punish: The Birth of the Prison*. New York: Vintage Books.

Green, Sarah. 2005. *Notes from the Balkans: Locating Marginality and Ambiguity on the Greek-Albanian Border*. Princeton: Princeton University Press.

Gutmann, Matthew C. 1996. *The Meanings of Macho: Being a Man in Mexico City*. Berkeley: University of California Press.

Lause, Mark A. 2009. *The Antebellum Crisis & America's First Bohemians*. Kent: Kent State University Press.

Meskimmon, Marsha. 2011. *Contemporary Art and the Cosmopolitan Imagination*. London/New York: Routledge.

Novak, David. 2010. Cosmopolitanism, Remediation, and the Ghost World of Bollywood. *Cultural Anthropology* 25 (1): 40–72.

Rapport, Nigel, and Ronald Stade. 2007. A Cosmopolitan Turn—Or Return? *Social Anthropology* 15 (2): 223–235.

Robbins, Bruce. 1998. Comparative Cosmopolitanisms. In *Cosmopolitics: Thinking and Feeling Beyond the Nation*, ed. Pheng Cheah and Bruce Robbins, 246–264. Minneapolis: University of Minnesota Press.

Rotenberg, Robert. 1995. The Metropolis and Everyday Life. In *Urban Life: Readings in Urban Anthropology*, ed. George Walter and Zenner Gmelch. Long Grove: Waveland Press.

Scheld, Suzanne. 2007. Youth Cosmopolitanism: Clothing, the City and Globalization in Dakar, Senegal. *City and Society* 19 (2): 232–253.

Tsing, Anna Lowenhaupt. 2005. *Friction: An Ethnography of Global Connections*. Princeton: Princeton University Press.

Velho, Gilberto. 2002. *A Utopia Urbana: Um Estudo de Antropologia Social*. Rio de Janeiro: Jorge Zahar Editor.

CHAPTER 6

Friends of Dusk and Dawn

Abstract The chapter deals with bohemians' intimate friendships that take place beyond the bounds of nocturnal bohemia and entail an unusual amount of attention to same-sex romances and sexual relationships. The chapter analyzes the kinds of practices and discourses that thrive in these kinds of friendships and considers how they structure and are structured by the bohemian community as well as mainstream society. By reserving talk about same-sex sexuality to intimate moments among close friends, bohemians are able to realize a specific politics of queerness that allows them the opportunity to construct lives for themselves that are not over determined by a fixed sexual identity. The chapter underscores how these fringe moments of intimacy ultimately work to sustain the bohemian community's queer form of cosmopolitan belonging.

Keywords Belonging • Intimacy • Same-sex desire • Gender/Sexual identity

Sunday afternoons tend to be the least eventful part of the week in Teresina. The sun feels hotter, movement seems slower, and silence sounds quieter. The heavy feeling of "*domingão*," or "Big Sunday," sets in, and lethargy takes over with its greatest force. Most stores are closed, and movement on the streets is next to nil. Hangovers plague a good many, and, for some, the mere thought of the coming workweek is enough to

© The Author(s) 2019
T. E. Murphy, *Queerly Cosmopolitan*,
https://doi.org/10.1007/978-3-030-00296-1_6

make one's head begin to ache. One week before Carnival, in 2009, Sérgio and Gustavo rescued me from such a domingão, by taking me to a Carnival parade.

Expressing enthusiasm about exposing me to more of what Carnival means to them, Sérgio and Gustavo explained that we were heading all the way to Mocambinho, a neighborhood well beyond downtown in the far reaches of the North Zone. Mocambinho is a vast neighborhood that has taken a course similar to a great number of other neighborhoods in the city. It began as a government-assisted housing development and has grown into a full-fledged neighborhood, complete with small, basic grocery stores, bars, churches, a few modest restaurants, and its own traditions. One such tradition, I would later discover, is the *Bloco da Farinha Seca* (the Dry Flour Parade). In the carnivalesque spirit of overturning the everyday, the parade is centered on throwing white flour or cornstarch at friends, family, and passers-by participating in the revelry. What Sérgio and Gustavo refrained from telling me was something else that would be integrated into this powdered frenzy: men of all ages, shapes, and sizes in drag, roaming about the neighborhood campily clad in housedresses and tousled wigs, donning slapdash makeup and toting dainty purses.

We arrived to Mocambinho just before sundown. We had a good hour to spare before the parade would start, and Sérgio suggested that we take a walk through the middle of the neighborhood to a little outdoor bar he and Gustavo knew about. Sérgio's suggestion came to me as a bit of a surprise. I had never taken a walk outside with either of them anywhere in Teresina before, let alone at night in a neighborhood that I had heard was particularly unsafe. As we proceeded along a dimly lit side street, Sérgio and Gustavo commented about how impressed they were with the rapid development of the neighborhood, pointing out details that often serve as good indicators of upward mobility in Brazil: freshly painted plaster-covered walls surrounding individual properties, electrically charged fences crowning the tops of some, native plants decorating and protecting others, an impressive number of roads made of stone, and a fair number of others paved with asphalt.

Once we arrived at the bar and began to cool off with a beer, Sérgio and Gustavo started telling me about what carnival means to them. Gustavo said, "There's no bigger excuse than Carnival. No one will make fun of you about what you did during Carnival." I responded, "So you never hear people say, 'Remember what *he* did last Carnival?'" "Never." Gustavo laughed and continued:

During Carnival, you're not allowed to think. You go crazy. You can have sex with one hundred people if you want and it doesn't matter. There's no judgment, no shame, no fear. *É só carne* (It's just flesh/meat)! Hell, you could even charge money for sex! There's no such thing as prostitution during Carnival!

Sérgio laughed and added, "It's true. You listen to music, wear clothes, and dance in ways that you would never do any other time of the year. Everyone just lets go." After sitting and talking for a while at the bar, three rowdy young men, probably in their early 20s, wearing dresses and carrying cans of beer passed in front of the bar. When more followed, including two who were holding hands, I turned to Gustavo and Sérgio and said, "Oh my!", causing them both to laugh. "Just wait, you'll see," Sérgio added.

Back on the main avenue, a few small truck-type floats (*trios elétricos*) were stopped in the road, blaring Carnival and Brazilian funk music, and a good number of people of various ages and appearances were soiled with white flour, dancing, laughing, and drinking beer and rum in the street and on the elevated sidewalk. Men in drag strolled hand in hand with their wives and girlfriends while families and friends stood on the sidelines pointing and laughing at them; a young man in a car tried to throw a few of his friends—who were wearing nothing but wigs, underwear, and flip-flops—off the top of his car by quickly accelerating and breaking; a small group of flamboyant *bichas* started play-fighting in the street and shouting *"BEEESHAAAA!"* at each other[1]; a middle-aged woman unscathed by the floury mess no sooner than passed in front of us before someone dowsed her with a face-full, causing her to turn and look at us in disbelief and then begin to laugh uncontrollably. A group of children and adults nearby roped the three of us into a well-known funk dance where someone gets pulled into the middle of the circle to grind their hips and circle them down over the top of a beer bottle. In a matter of minutes, a man wearing a giant wig pulled me into the circle and placed the bottle on the ground between my legs. When I looked to my

---

[1] *Bicha* refers to a gay man but has no adequate translation in English. Unlike *viado*, which probably translates best into English as "fag/faggot" and is used most often by nonqueer people as a derogatory term for such men, *bicha*—literally meaning "female animal"—is employed in communities of same-sex desire throughout Brazil, connoting the effeminate "nature" or performances of gender/sexuality of gay men.

friends for help, they said, "You have to do it! It will be much worse if you don't!" And so I gave it my best, swirling my hips down over the bottle, all the while remembering my friends' mantra, "You can do it all! It's Carnival!"

As the festivities began to wind down, we started heading for the car, when Gustavo spotted an older man in a dress stumbling around in the street by himself. Gustavo began joking with him by asking him what was inside his purse. The man opened it and turned it upside down revealing nothing. We all chuckled. Then he mumbled that he was trying to find himself a man. Gustavo, incredulous, asked the man, "Do you like men?" The man affirmed with slurred speech, "*Gosto de TUUU-DOOOO*" ("I like EVERYTHING"). Gustavo chatted with him for a second and then caught back up with us. "You guys, he's gay! Can you believe it? A humble man, of that age, in this neighborhood?" "He's not gay, Gustavo. It's just Carnival!" Then, as we turned a corner, three guys sitting on the curb stopped talking and looked up at us passing by. One of them said something to the others loud enough so that we could hear them. After we passed them, Sérgio turned to me and said, "Did you hear what they said? They said, 'If we only had a car.' I'm pretty sure that was a subtext, as if to suggest that if we had a car, they'd be willing to take a ride with us." Sérgio winked. "I love Carnival," said Gustavo. "If only we didn't have to work tomorrow!" Sérgio whined.

As we drove home, we bonded over the great time we had, talking about how many attractive men were there that seemed to be willing to do anything. Sérgio told us that a few years prior he had gone to a similar parade with our friend Caio, only in a different neighborhood. He told us that he and Caio sat on the curb watching two strong and handsome macho men in the street. Both were extremely drunk, wearing only short wigs, lipstick, short skirts, and flip-flops. They were holding hands, kissing, and roughly grabbing each other. At some point, one of them became distracted by an attractive woman passing by, and all of the sudden, the other, appearing jealous, punched him in the face. Both men began throwing punches at one another other, but within minutes, Sérgio attested, the two were back in one another's arms, kissing and stroking each other's wigs. Sérgio said that he and Caio still today like to joke about how that image remains one of their greatest sexual fantasies.

DUSK AND DAWN

As I demonstrate in Chap. 4, as a community the galera[2] appears most integrated at night through its nocturnal bohemia. A refuge from the oppressive heat and normative light of day, night becomes a space of possibility where all kinds of life are given the chance to thrive and go unnoticed by mainstream society. Still there are other moments—ones that I refer to here as "dusk and dawn"—that serve a number of participants in the galera a different purpose. Dusk and dawn are like Carnival in that they give many members of the galera room to breathe desires that are given little airtime in the milieux of nocturnal bohemia, their families, and "daylife" more generally. Dusk and dawn open up a space for close friends not only to share stories of hookups with same-sex partners but also to theorize same-sex desire more generally and situate themselves in terms of such theorizations. Many close friends who experience same-sex desire come together in the late afternoon, after fulfilling their obligations with work and family, and in the early morning—accompanying one another home after nocturnal bohemia. Dusk and dawn are spaces of trust not only because they involve discussions about one another's sexual desires (which is often considered personal, if not secret, information) but also because close friends are sometimes exposed to one another at their most vulnerable moments. Dusk and dawn friends may know where you live, how much money you don't have, and who you are secretly sleeping with. They may hear about your family problems, know about your vices, discover who you pray to, and learn about your dreams and fears. Most notably, dusk and dawn friends establish a sense of belonging for one another by forging a special space to talk through and make sense of their same-sex desires and relationships.

In-between Space

The trip to the Carnival parade in Mocambinho with Sérgio and Gustavo was rather typical of the kinds of intimate moments that I experienced with various participants in the galera. These moments sometimes occur

---

[2] The "galera" refers to the clique of people who come together to form Teresina's nocturnal bohemia (Chap. 4).

just after sharing pineapple at the edge of the river at sunset. Other times they happen at bars and in cars. They often happen when a few close friends regularly meet at someone's home before heading off to a *festa* (party) like High Jinx. In such cases, hosts do not hesitate to answer their doors half dressed, invite close friends to come in and help themselves to beers in the freezer, and proceed to shuffle around the house getting ready; before heading out, friends sometimes sit around for a couple of hours, chatting, laughing, and even dancing around the house or apartment. If heading to a costume party, close friends will convene in a bedroom—air-conditioning or fan cranked way up—putting makeup on one another and goofing around getting into character. Sometimes these in-between spaces materialize in transit—cropping up in a car on the way to or on the way home from an event. Other times, they manifest after a festa while seated outside a gas station, sprawled out on a concrete bench in a deserted plaza, or on the patio of a burger joint as the sky begins to lighten.

The marginal position that these friendly exchanges take up in time, space, and social life contribute to their intimate character—they are sites in which particular topics of conversation often considered to be "out of place" in other realms of life are given their due. Overwhelmingly, for participants in the galera with whom I became best acquainted with during fieldwork, dusk and dawn involved discussions of one another's same-sex desires, sexual practices, and sexual/romantic relationships.[3] With the highly restricted norms around gender/sexuality of Teresina's status-conscious upwardly mobile mainstream (see Chap. 3), its GLS culture,[4] and the institution of the family, many participants in the galera who experience same-sex desire depend on these other spaces and times to narrate and negotiate their same-sex desires.

---

[3] It is widely accepted that numerous participants in the galera do not engage in same-sex sex or romantic relationships. However, because the majority does, and because I was most directly exposed to such participants, I have come to see these intimate moments in terms of a shared subjectivity around same-sex desire. Indeed, intimate moments exist among close friends who share opposite-sex desires as well as those who do not share sexual desires. However, such moments are not my focus here.

[4] As I explain in Chap. 4, GLS is an acronym that came out of an identity politics movement to institutionalize gay spaces as not exclusively "*Gay*" or "*Lesbica*," but also "S," which stands for "*simpatizantes*," or "sympathizers."

Hookup Stories

Recounting the details of hookups is typical of the kinds of intimate moments that dusk and dawn friends share. Stories of "hooking up" ("*ficando*") with same-sex partners come in all shapes and sizes. Some serve to unite friends around a shared past or the current state of affairs in terms of opportunities for hooking up, while others allow friends to more fully realize secret and even scandalous encounters that must otherwise be kept hush-hush.

Reminiscing about how hooking up worked in the past, some friends talk about meeting same-sex love interests and sexual partners clandestinely via a local phone service and chat rooms online. Some women recall how finding a same-sex partner once required frequenting predominantly lesbian bars full of "dykes who play ball and drink cachaça" or attending regular concerts put on by Dandinha—a well-known local female singer—that, while perhaps not obvious to all attendees, always attracted more than a handful of women seeking other women. Men and women both talk about the time before their involvement in the galera when they would meet sexual/romantic interests at Boca da Noite—a weekly music event downtown that was relatively unrestricted to any one particular gender or sexual identity.

The current state of affairs around hooking up is an equally salient topic of conversation. Friends comment how technologies such as Fotolog, Orkut, Facebook, Twitter, Twitpic, Formspring, and MSN Instant Messenger offer more strategies for meeting than ever before. Some women say they are happy to see an increasing number of other like-minded women in terms of gender presentation and lifestyle at GLS bars and festas. Other friends talk about how they don't like to hook up with people who take part in the GLS culture or the galera despite the changes taking place in these communities.

Dusk and dawn friends enjoy sharing stories with one another about secret and sometimes scandalous hookups. Some tell stories of exchanging suggestive glances and even phone numbers with potential sex partners who are accompanied by husbands, wives, boyfriends, or girlfriends in locales as public as the shopping malls. Some male friends report to one another how at different times of day and different places in the city men can have impromptu sexual encounters with nongay-identified men. Still others share stories about their same-sex sexual encounters at particular social venues typically thought to be hyper-heterosexual, in which they are able to discreetly flirt and hook up with nongay-identified women and men of a variety of social standings.

THEORIZING SAME-SEX DESIRE

In a context where once taken-for-granted notions of gender/sexuality are in crisis, dusk and dawn make room for close friends to theorize conflicting understandings of gender/sexuality. As particular notions of gender/sexuality thought to be "local" on the one hand, come into dialogue with those thought to be "foreign" on the other hand, many Teresinenses struggle to make sense of contradictions that arise with these intersecting discourses of gender/sexuality (Parker 1999a; Manalansan 2003; Boellstorff 2005, Donham 1998). For participants in the galera who experience same-sex desire, dusk and dawn are an antidote.

Throughout Brazil, opposite-sex desire has long proved fundamental to gender norms—a reality observable in both public discourse and practices. Not only are women and men assumed to desire persons of the opposite sex, they are also expected to engage in public displays of that desire. Women, both young and old, face pressure to conform to national conventions around femininity and beauty that are considered suitable for the male gaze. Such pressure to conform to gender norms has all but dwindled in Teresina's fierce climate of socioeconomic change and residents' growing preoccupation with social status. From the time that they are young, men are made aware of the fact that their masculinity is tightly bound to their sexual experiences with women and voicing their love for the female body. It is still not unheard of for fathers in Teresina to take their sons to a brothel to initiate them into manhood by paying for them to have sex with a sex worker. And whether in conversations with male taxi drivers or my female bosses and coworkers at the language school, I was often asked about my opinion about Brazilian women's bodies and the number of Brazilian girlfriends I have had.

No sooner than discovering the importance of keeping up appearances in Teresina did I realize that what it means to be a man and a woman is far more complex than I had originally thought. Masculinity is not only based on men's ability to sexually conquer and dominate women, nor is it understood uniformly by Teresinenses. Femininity is contingent upon a woman's social standing and, just as it is the case with men, sexual practices do not always directly correspond with a woman's public gender/sexual identity. Perhaps most interestingly, over time I found that dusk and dawn were not merely spaces where close friends could safely and comfortably discuss their same-sex desires and practices, but also make sense of local contradictions around gender and sexuality and their own subjectivities in relation to them.

Sexuality and Social Standing

One pervasive belief among Teresina's status-conscious upwardly mobile residents is that gays and lesbians could not possibly be of any social position other than lower or lower-middle class. I initially found such a notion perplexing—how could social class determine one's sexual desire? Mariel and Fernanda enlightened me on the matter one early morning over bread and coffee at Mariel's apartment after a long night out. The two had been lamenting about how difficult it is to find available like-minded women to date in Teresina. As Fernanda pulled out a cigarette, propped up her bare feet up on a chair, and tossed her hard pack of Carltons on the table, she explained:

> They (participants in Teresina's upwardly-mobile mainstream society) don't believe that people with 'social class' *se entenda* (experience and recognize their same-sex desire) because they see this as a defect or weakness. They think, 'how could a girl, who is well raised and who studied at a good school run by nuns, be lesbian'?

Mariel, lounging in a beanbag chair in only a sports bra and a pair of men's boxer shorts, added that such upwardly mobile people view same-sex desire as a psychological problem that any family with "social class" would remedy. Fernanda explains that it is not so much that a woman's elevated socioeconomic status would result in her ceasing to desire other women; rather, she would be more apt to abandon her public identity as a lesbian. Both Fernanda and Mariel attest that mainstream associations between lower economic status and same-sex desire prevent many women from pursuing other women for fear of downward class mobility. As a result, Fernanda and Mariel both have found themselves flirting in public and online with married middle-class women and occasionally hooking up with them on the sly.

Men who assume a gay public identity are also widely associated with the lower echelons of Teresina's economic spectrum. As scholars like Peter Fry (1983) and Richard Parker (1999a) among others have pointed out, in rural and lower-class urban Brazil, overwhelmingly a man's masculinity is based on assuming the insertive (*activo*) role in the sex act regardless of the object he penetrates (female, male, etc.). Accordingly, only males who take a receptive (*passivo*) role in the sex act with other men are marked as deviant. This system of gender/sexuality creates a world in which men (*homens*) are differentiated from bichas, the latter of which are thought to assume a somewhat effeminate gender presentation and are not considered "real men" (*"homens de verdade"*). Bichas occupy a place in rural and lower-class urban life that, while marginal, is recognized and not thought to be terribly uncommon. In Teresina's upwardly mobile mainstream society, however, there is little room for bichas. If upwardly mobile men have same-sex desires and/or act on them (regardless of the role they take in the act), they are expected to keep such matters to themselves. Therefore, because participants in the galera are all from middle-class families, those who experience same-sex desire are threatened not only by being seen as deviant in terms of gender/sexuality but also as having a lower socioeconomic status. Especially within the broader context of Teresina's socially conservative and status-conscious mainstream society, the opportunity to discuss and critique associations between same-sex desire and low economic status with like-minded individuals is to forge a sense of belonging around a shared middle-class subjectivity of same-sex desire.

Over a beer one evening at an outdoor bar on the edge of the Poti River after work, my friend Walter—an accounting student in his late 20s who does some designing on the side—began talking about his friends at the private university where he studies.

> All of my male friends there are heterosexual. I bet many of them have hooked up with other men. I've already played around with some of them. I even had sex with one of them after a concert. In the morning when he was sober, he told me that it was fun but that he didn't want it to happen again because he doesn't like men. To be honest, I never imagined that it could have happened with him. But it's true. Here, the majority of men have sex with men.

From personal experiences, Walter—like many men and women in the galera—believes that many people engage in same-sex sex regardless of their social class—a belief that is reinforced by friends' discussions of experimenting with sexuality at a young age. Juliana talks about how growing up in the countryside caused her to be extremely curious and willing to experiment with almost anything, including but not limited to having sex with her female cousin during her yearly visits from Brasília. Likewise, Gustavo recalls visiting his aunt on the countryside when he was young. His male cousins and neighbors would regularly hide up in a mango tree on the property and watch one another masturbate. Sometimes these "games" would extend into one-on-one experiences between him and a neighbor or a cousin in which they would secretly have sex—occurrences that, at least for a few of them, lasted into the boys' teenage years. While many men and women in Teresina may have experienced or continue to engage in same-sex sexual practices, far fewer appear to assume a sexual identity or subjectivity that reflects such practices.

One Saturday evening on our way to meet Raquel at a bar in the East Zone, Sérgio and I happened to drive through a small segment of downtown where a handful of male sex workers (*michês*) often work. As we traversed the deserted streets, we passed through an intersection where a strikingly handsome man in a baseball cap standing near a corner was smiling at us. Sérgio and I immediately turned and looked at one another. Beginning to laugh, Sérgio threw the car in reverse and pulled up alongside the man to make small talk and confirm that he was hustling. Sérgio told him that we were off to meet up with a friend but ended the conversation by making sure that the man is usually at that same spot at on Saturday nights. As I watched the whole interaction, I couldn't help but notice not so much the man's masculine posture but rather his big smile and unusual air of confidence. Once we drove away, I asked Sérgio how these men make sense of what they do.

> It's all justified in the money or the beer that's gained. He tells himself that he's doing it for gain—to make money, to get drunk, and to get some pleasure. It's like that with all guys who fuck guys who don't consider themselves gay, not just michês. Any guys who don't do it for beer or money have to do it secretly and have more difficulty doing it. Some michês think their life is better than being gay. They get money and sex and they like it.

Dusk and dawn friends recognize that sexual desires, practices, and identities are not reducible to social class. Instead, the importance of maintaining one's social status—how one is seen and understood by others—shapes what people do with their "deviant" desires. Over cokes and savory pastries one evening at a table tucked away from the flow of shoppers in the mall, a few intimate friends from the galera chatted about how some men in Teresina maintain their social position despite their same-sex desires. Júnior commented:

> People have more chances to be themselves here in Teresina than in the countryside. There you have to hide who you are. Here there is more anonymity. For example, those who have more money drive to the periphery of the city and pay to have sex with a guy. Those who have less money will assume a gay identity more easily.

Júnior's comment echoes Fernanda's interpretation: not only is money thought to rid people of psychological "problems" like gender/sexual deviance, money becomes a mechanism for concealing such desires.

Other friends commented on the problem of same-sex desire in maintaining one's status. Carlinhos told me about a middle-class guy he used to date named Eduardo. Carlinhos explained that Eduardo used to model and was quite effeminate. Once his parents started suspecting that he might be gay, they told him that they would take his car away until he got a girlfriend. Eduardo obeyed and now he has his car back; he also continues to date and have sex with men—only now he is more discreet about it. I asked Carlinhos if Eduardo's effeminate behavior causes people to doubt his heterosexuality. Carlinhos responded, "Of course, but what matters is that he has a girlfriend. That's what's most important." The lifestyle that Eduardo currently maintains is not unlike other stories I have heard close friends talk about: from designers to doctors to business owners to politicians to one's own mother or father, numerous people in Teresina are thought to experience and act on their same-sex desires while maintaining a heterosexual public image. My friend Tiago also illustrates the importance of maintaining a heterosexual appearance through a saying that he loves to repeat: "*Mulher não gosta de homem, não! Quem gosta de homem é viado. Mulher só gosta de dinheiro*" ("Women don't like men! Fags like men. Women only like money"). While the saying connotes a number of cultural values, central to it is the notion that marriage is not only about love and sexual desire. Instead, the real purpose of marriage is an arrangement that confers status and approval from one's family and mainstream society. This belief comes out of the notion that a man should marry a woman for her virtuosity rather than her sexual prowess. If a man marries a woman who is "good in bed," he is sure to become a *corno* (the unfortunate partner of an unfaithful woman), emasculating him and ultimately soiling his reputation. Therefore, a wise man marries a woman who, at the very least, is guaranteed to maintain his status position if not elevate it, and, thus, seeks sexual pleasure elsewhere. It is in pursuit of such desires that *namoradas* (lovers), *putas* (female sex workers), *michês* (male sex workers), *travestis* (trans female sex workers), and bichas come in handy.

Competing Understandings of Sexuality

Dusk and dawn also provide a space for participants to theorize sexuality and understand themselves through discussions of what appear to be contradictory understandings of sexuality. The existence of what Richard

Parker (1999b) identifies as two different "systems of sexual classification" (Parker 1999b: 257) of male same-sex sexuality in Brazil is common knowledge for many Brazilians, including participants in the galera. They are well aware that some men who have sex with men in Teresina do not consider themselves gay because they operate on what Parker calls the "popular system of sexual classification" (Parker 1999b: 257) in which only the man assuming the "passivo" role in the sex act (bicha) is marked. Equally, participants in the galera are familiar with what Richard Parker terms the "medical/scientific system of sexual classification" (Parker 1999b: 257) espoused by sexual identity politics movements in Brazil and much of the world in which one's object of sexual desire (rather than role in the sex act) determines one's sexuality—that is, men who desire men are gay and women who desire women are lesbian. But because, as Parker asserts (Parker 1999b: 257), this latter system has come to mark only men taking the "passivo" role (i.e., bichas), many men who take the "activo" role in sex with men in places like Teresina (on the periphery of Brazil's dominant urban areas) do not consider themselves gay. In other words, while terms like "*gay*" and "*homossexual*" are commonly used in Brazil, in many contexts they are considered to be synonymous with the (lower-class and rural) identity of the "bicha"—a tendency that further reinforces same-sex desire's association with people of lower socioeconomic status.[5] Dusk and dawn friends are privy to all kinds of experiences and stories around same-sex sex in Teresina, the Northeast, and Brazil in general, and understand quite well that these "systems," as Parker points out, do not adequately represent the complexity of the lived experiences around same-sex desire (Parker 1999b: 257).

Sérgio, for example, says that he saw an interview on television with a Brazilian psychologist who said that *entendidas* (women who recognize their same-sex desires but do not necessarily act on them) are not lesbian, whereas *entendidos* (men who recognize their same-sex desires regardless of acting on them) are gay. In other words, female homosexuality is based

---

[5] It is important to note that many Teresinenses who employ participants in the galera for their avant-garde aesthetic expertise are not oblivious to the fact that some of these men and women engage in same-sex practices and relationships. It is even possible that this knowledge contributes to clients' confidence in their employees' ability to execute the task at hand. Be that as it may, many clients still consider it out of place for their employees to be overly explicit about their same-sex desires. At the end of the day, it is important for many clients that their employees maintain a respectable middle-class public image, which leaves little room for nonnormative gender/sexual identities.

on the experience of same-sex sex and male homosexuality is based on same-sex desire alone. Antonio recounts a story involving an explanation offered by a different psychologist. A young man named Douglas that Antonio used to hook up with once went to a psychologist because he was concerned that he might be gay. The psychologist asked him if he had ever taken the receptive role in the sex act with another man. When he responded "No," the psychologist told him that he had nothing to worry about, for only men who "*dar cu*" ("give their ass") to other men are gay.

Carlinhos, Júnior, and Gustavo have different takes on the matter. Carlinhos believes that only men who experience love for other men are gay, whereas men who have sex with men are just regular homens. He relies on this distinction to make sense of the difference between him and his four brothers, all of whom, he has learned from third parties, have had sex with other men. Carlinhos says he is gay because, unlike his brothers, he feels affection for men and dreams of having a long-term relationship with another man. His brothers are not gay because they are happily married and love women. According to Carlinhos, homens have sex with bichas and travestis for the same reason that little boys in the countryside penetrate other boys and even animals—to experience pleasure and to feel powerful. Boys who grow up learning that to be a man is to dominate by penetrating in general, and then go on to love and eventually marry women in particular, are the epitome of what it means to be a homem, he says. Carlinhos' theory, however, omits something: would such men still be considered homens if they were to let another homem penetrate them? Júnior includes such a possibility in his formulation. Júnior uses the somewhat tongue-in-cheek invented term, "*hetero-passivo*" ("penetrated male heterosexual") to refer to homens who do not love other men but are willing to take the passivo role in the sex act with other men. Though Júnior knows people often use the term jokingly, he says he believes that it holds water. Sex is just sex, he claims. Who you love says more about who you are. Júnior and Carlinhos defend their position with the example of another participant in the galera named Igor. Known to date women but to hook up with men on occasion, Igor was thought to be gay only after he began an exclusive relationship with Paulo. Now that he has a boyfriend, the two explain, Igor is gay. Gustavo vehemently disagrees with both positions held by Carlinhos and Júnior. Espousing the so-called medical/scientific system of classification in which one's object of desire (sexual or affective or both) is what determines sexuality, Gustavo believes if a woman desires a female-bodied person in any way, she is lesbian, and likewise, a man who desires a male-bodied person is gay.

Thus, while the galera's politics is queer in the sense that it leaves room for fluidity and experimentation without the threat of being ascribed a sexual identity, individuals have their own opinions and understandings about gender/sexuality that they are able to share and negotiate in intimate contexts with close friends who also experience same-sex desire. But what sense can be made of the variety of understandings of sexuality that arise in discussions among dusk and dawn friends? Not only do a number of friends disagree about what it is that makes a woman lesbian or a man gay, their stories suggests that a similar ambiguity around understandings of gender/sexuality is also prevalent in Teresina's mainstream society. Might not such an amalgamation of understandings around gender/sexuality relate to the role of the private-public distinction that Richard Parker (1999b) argues is central to erotic experiences in Brazil? Parker elucidates:

> Whether 'within four walls', 'beneath the sheets', or in any other situation in which one is somehow 'concealed' or even 'disguised', it is possible to encounter a freedom of sexual expression that would be explicitly prohibited in the 'outside', 'public' world. In the freedom of such private, hidden moments, Brazilians suggest, anything can happen, everything is possible (Parker 1991, 1992). (Parker 1999b: 259)

In other words—and as numerous conversations about sexuality among dusk and dawn friends have pointed out—in many cases, there is a sharp distinction between the sex people engage in and the public gender/sexual identity they assume. Parker further elaborates:

> Within this world, which is focused on private as opposed to public meanings, the significance of sexual practices takes shape less as an expression of an overriding system of sexual classification based less on activity/passivity, sexual object choice and so on, than as an end in itself. It does not centre on one's identity, on some inner truth of the sexual self, but on *tesão* (sexual excitement) and *prazer* (pleasure). (Parker 1999b: 259)

It would make sense, then, in a world in which public identities do not necessarily correspond with erotic practices that a variety of understandings of sexuality and gender/sexual identity would abound. By sharing personal stories about same-sex desires, dusk and dawn friendships help make sense of this ambiguity.

SPACES OF SUBJECT FORMATION

Expressions of both opposite-sex and same-sex desires are not unusual at galera events or in other interactions among participants. Open displays of affection of both types of desires are often conspicuous in nocturnal bohemia; some participants occasionally disclose sexual/romantic interests in Twitter tweets and Facebook posts; and a handful of opposite-sex and same-sex couples are almost always involved in the galera. However, as I have attempted to show, as I became better acquainted with individual participants, I often found myself in situations where same-sex desires and the implications of these desires (romantic/sexual relationships, hookups, familial relations, gender/sexual identity, discrimination, employment, etc.) were the topic of conversation. Over time, I began to notice that by and large this *talk* of same-sex sex and sexuality—except for the occasional comment about a potential hookup for the night—rarely took place in the spaces and events that comprise nocturnal bohemia (festas, bazaars, performances, etc.).

Nocturnal bohemia is one of the galera's most visible manifestations of the community, and because of its ethos of queerness, one might be inclined to think that it would be an ideal context for participants to openly articulate their same-sex desires. This, however, is not the case. In fact, it is *because* of the galera's politics of queerness (fluidity, flexibility, and openness) around identity and community that such talk of participants' same-sex desires is not given greater importance in nocturnal bohemia. As I elaborate in greater detail in Chap. 4, "queerness" as I use it with regard to the galera should not be mistaken for the prevalent usage of the term in which "queer" stands in for the LGBT community. The queerness that characterizes the galera greatly exceeds and challenges such a notion.

I interpret the galera as queer in no less than two ways: the first is queer-as-nonnormative, meaning that participants in the galera together find refuge in ways of life that thrive at the margins of mainstream society, be they explicitly related to sexuality or not; it is also in this sense that the galera may be seen to operate along the lines of a "queer temporality" (Halberstam 2005). The second notion of queerness is queer-as-unbound, meaning that participants rely on the galera for cultivating a self that is unbound, in flux, flexible, and unrestricted by any notion of a fixed identity. Although in nocturnal bohemia, same-sex desire is expressed and tolerated, if not celebrated, it is not given more importance than a number of other desires and their manifestations—for example, taste in music, dance, and gender presentation. Furthermore, because the galera's bohemia is generally centered on events like festas, concerts, performances, and bazaars, it does not provide a context particularly conducive to intimate discussions about one's sex life—for example, music tends to be loud and participants tend to be more interested in engaging in the task at hand, whether it be dancing, deejaying, performing, or watching a performance. When conversations *are* had in nocturnal bohemia, they tend to be more about the aesthetics and workings of the event or gossip about attendees than about individuals' sexual experiences, desires, or subjectivities. One particular bohemian's experience with the galera illustrates this dynamic quite well.

Jacob, a participant in his mid-20s, told me that he found himself engaging in nocturnal bohemia when he started dating Marcelo—one of the galera's central figures at the time. Jacob grew up downtown, studied at one of the newer and less prestigious private high schools in town, was something of a jock, loved to dance and listen to forró,[6] and, like the majority of his friends, had dreams of becoming a lawyer. Shortly after his first sexual experience with another man, he met Marcelo online and the two began to date. In the beginning, Jacob kept his relationship a secret from his family and friends (all of whom he assumes to be heterosexual), but word eventually got out. His mother was supportive for the most part, but the majority of Jacob's friends and some family members refused to accept his new lifestyle. Through Marcelo, Jacob became friends with numerous participants in the galera and gradually began to feel like he fit in. After nearly three years of being together, however, the couple broke up and Jacob began testing out GLS spaces in Teresina in the hopes of acquiring a new partner. Because Marcelo was Jacob's first boyfriend, prior to their breakup the only community Jacob was familiar with in which same-sex desire was tolerated was the galera. While Teresina's GLS culture seemed to be a logical alternative to the galera, in the end Jacob identified more with the galera's nocturnal bohemia. Unlike the GLS spaces he frequented, which he found to be largely centered on finding someone to hook up with, the galera allowed him to enjoy himself in ways that did not necessarily pertain to his same-sex desire. Jacob told me:

[6] Forró is a genre of traditional northeastern music whose base components are the accordion, a special drum, and a metal triangle.

With Marcelo, I was born again. I started seeing myself as gay. I started observing men more, going out more. But when we broke up, I didn't want to keep Marcelo's friends. I wanted my own friends. I needed time and space. I would go to the gay bar and Marcelo hated that place. When people found out that we had broken up, they wanted to hook up with me. But then I got tired of it. I wanted something more interesting, more underground, more interesting people, cool people.

After Marcelo landed himself a new boyfriend and stopped going out as often, Jacob began reacquainting himself with the galera's nightlife.

While Jacob's involvement in the galera via Marcelo helped him develop a subjectivity around his same-sex desire, it also offered him room to experiment and explore aspects of himself that extended beyond his sexuality. In other words, nocturnal bohemia exposed him to new kinds of aesthetics (music, dancing, etc.) and people that he found stimulating without the need to act on or address his same-sex desire. Indeed, Jacob's same-sex desire is far from out of place in nocturnal bohemia; the difference is that unlike the GLS spaces he temporarily frequented, his sexuality is not the necessary focus of his nights out with the galera. Jacob is not alone in initially becoming incorporated into the galera through a same-sex partner. Many men and women of a variety of ages, professions, and middle-class backgrounds have become acquainted with the galera via same-sex relationships, whether short-lived or long lasting. That said, while same-sex desire may, in this sense, underpin a fair amount of the galera's formation as a community, it still remains but one aspect of its identity.

As I have demonstrated in previous chapters, for participants in the galera to carve out an authentic world and sense of belonging for themselves, they set themselves apart from mainstream society both in discourse (e.g., "mafrense" and "chique") and practice (e.g., nocturnal bohemia). Teresina's GLS subculture and the LGBT identity politics movement— like in most large cities in Brazil—have gained a significant amount of attention from the media and have developed their own sets of standards and norms. While women and men who experience same-sex desire still face discrimination in Teresina, and, as a group, remain on the margins of mainstream society, institutions centered on same-sex desire are seen by many participants in the galera as less than ideal for establishing community and a sense of belonging. This is not to say that all participants completely reject the GLS culture or the LGBT identity politics movement.

Occasionally some participants attend, deejay, or report on Teresina's GLS and LGBT events. Yet because these institutions challenge men and women's ability to construct a world in which they are seen and see themselves as something more than subjects of same-sex desire, many participants take refuge in the galera because it is a world in which one's same-sex desire is accepted but does not overshadow other interests and axes of identification (e.g., aesthetic tastes, political views, and practices).

CONCLUSION: DUSK AND DAWN AS CARNIVAL

By largely reserving talk about same-sex sexuality to intimate moments among close friends, dusk and dawn can be seen to contribute to the sustenance of the galera's overall queerness. A specific politics of queerness is able to be realized, specific alliances can be forged that may be less likely otherwise (e.g., friendships among people who do not share the same sexual desires), and participants are given the opportunity to construct lives for themselves that are not overdetermined by a sexual identity. Conversely, these intimate spaces may be seen to sustain the normative character of daily life in Teresina. Rather than attempting to upset mainstream conventions around gender/sexuality, the majority of participants in the galera who experience same-sex desire are relatively discrete if not somewhat "covert" about their sexuality in the limelight of public life (Newton 1972: 23). As such, these fringe spaces of intimacy work to sustain the galera's queer ethos of belonging.

In a sense, dusk and dawn are not unlike Carnival. Carnival is an inversion of the everyday, an exceptional time and space standing apart from quotidian life, a temporary suspension in which virtually anything can happen—the events detailed at the beginning of this chapter serve as a case in point. Still, scholars like Roberto DaMatta (1991) have argued that Carnival is integral to the prevailing social fabric of Brazilian society. Writing with regard to Carnival and other rituals in Brazil, DaMatta asserts, "rituals must not be taken as events that are essentially different (in form, quality, and substance) from those which constitute and inform the so-called routine of daily life" (DaMatta 1991: 53). According to DaMatta, the inversion that takes place during Carnival brings to the surface that which is excluded from the everyday. In a similar vein, the kinds of activities, personal information, and secrets that dusk and dawn friends share allow other realms of life to remain intact and separate. Dusk and dawn are also like Carnival in that they are spaces in which friends are able to let loose and be vulnerable before one another in expressing personal and socially taboo aspects of their lives. Like Carnival, there is no shame in these intimate moments; what happens in them remains in them and does not define those who participate in them. And while dusk and dawn are not entirely distinct from the galera community, mainstream society, and the family, the frequency and separate character of these moments suggest that, like Carnival, they serve to reinforce the overall structure of daily life for many participants.

But what are the effects of living in a world in which a yearly ritual serves as a continual reminder of both the normative structure of daily life as well as the possibility that things could be otherwise? Not only does it seem likely that practices permitted only during Carnival would sometimes spill over into other moments throughout the year, but also that thinking about the world in terms of stable, essential categories wouldn't hold much water. In this sense, Carnival may be seen to further support Richard Parker's (1999b) claim that the sexual practices a person enjoys in private do not necessarily correspond to her public identity. And like the old man who can put on a dress, tote a tiny purse, and flirt with men during Carnival, dusk and dawn and the same-sex desires that structure them do not make you who you are, they are just something you do.

REFERENCES

Boellstorff, Tom. 2005. *The Gay Archipelago: Sexuality and Nation in Indonesia*. Princeton: Princeton University Press.

DaMatta, Roberto. 1991. *Carnivals, Rogues, and Heroes: An Interpretation of the Brazilian Dilemma*. Notre Dame: University of Notre Dame Press.

Donham, Donald. 1998. Freeing South Africa: The "Modernization" of Male-Male Sexuality in Soweto. *Cultural Anthropology* 13 (1): 1–19.

Fry, Peter, and Edward McRae. 1983. *O Que É Homossexualidade?* São Paulo: Brasiliense.

Halberstam, Judith. 2005. *In a Queer Time and Place: Transgender Bodies, Subcultural Lives*. New York: New York University Press.

Manalansan, Martin F.I.V. 2003. *Global Divas: Filipino Gay Men in the Diaspora*. Durham: Duke University Press.

Newton, Esther. 1972. *Mother Camp: Female Impersonators in America*. Chicago: University of Chicago Press.

Parker, Richard. 1999a. *Beneath the Equator: Cultures of Desire, Male Homosexuality, and Emerging Gay Communities in Brazil*. London: Routledge.
———. 1999b. 'Within Four Walls': Brazilian Sexual Culture and HIV/AIDS. In *Culture, Society and Sexuality: A Reader*, ed. Richard Parker and Peter Aggleton. London: UCL Press.

CHAPTER 7

Epilogue: Queerness as Belonging

Abstract Beginning with a story about a conflict between the local minister of culture and a group of performance artists in Teresina, the epilogue ties the book's chapters together. It underscores the notion that in a place undergoing acute transformation like Teresina, rather than relying on a fixed or static identity, participants in alternative communities can establish a sense of belonging both in the world and at home by creatively maneuvering in and out of different subjectivities in a diversity of contexts and on numerous geographic scales.

Keywords Belonging • Urbanization • Queerness • Identity

Thinking back, it was a rather strange time to start working with the Atelier. The collective of performance artists had recently found itself embroiled in a conflict with its primary source of funding: the local government. As far as members of the Atelier saw it, the conflict was over opposing understandings of "culture" in Teresina. The Atelier is based in one of Teresina's largest and most marginalized neighborhoods. Several participants in the galera[1] had taken part in the group since its formation in 2006, and I had attended a handful of their performances on my trips

---

[1] The "galera" refers to the clique of people who come together to form Teresina's nocturnal bohemia (Chap. 4).

© The Author(s) 2019
T. E. Murphy, *Queerly Cosmopolitan*,
https://doi.org/10.1007/978-3-030-00296-1_7

143

to Teresina before conducting fieldwork. Not long after arriving in 2009, I reached out to the Atelier to see how I could become involved. Yuri, who I had gotten to know over the years through the galera, was very receptive to my interest and invited me to come to the theater the following morning.

When I arrived, a ballerina I knew named Luciana came running outside to pull me out of the sun and into a small, hot-pink office, into which Yuri and several others were crowded. In the middle of venting his frustrations, Yuri looked over at me and said with a smile in fluent English, "Hey. Come on in. Sorry. We're kind of in the middle of a mess here." Between brief exchanges in English with a man named Pedro about what I was doing there, I observed a woman named Sheila updating the Atelier's website as Yuri repeatedly dialed the number of the local cultural foundation, voicing his disbelief that an employer would ignore its employees' calls. Suddenly, Yuri uttered, "*Ja chega, gente! Eu não aguento mais.*" ["That's enough, guys! I can't take it anymore."]

Sheila rounded everyone up, and we relocated to a large rehearsal room where about 25 men and women—most of whom were in their 20s—formed a circle on the floor. Yuri and Sheila announced that unfortunately things were still up in the air as they still were unable to speak with the foundation, and that the most important thing to focus on was their weekly improvisational performance taking place that night.

For the next two hours, the group engaged in a heated discussion around the role of the audience, the nature of the spectacle, and the importance of establishing a relationship with the audience that falls somewhere between catering to it and disregarding it completely. Given the Atelier's tendency to engage in highly experimental art forms that sometimes confuse, disturb, or simply challenge audiences, this discussion seemed fitting—a point that became even clearer to me later when I learned more about the conflict with the local government.

After deciding on a theme for that evening's performance and formulating a rehearsal plan for the afternoon, we broke for lunch. I thanked Yuri and hopped into Luciana's car with Pedro. The three of us headed into the East Zone for an air-conditioned vegetarian lunch at Riverside mall.

The two caught me up to speed about the conflict in the car and over lunch. The local cultural foundation responsible for funding the building of the theater and employing the members of the Atelier had recently changed presidents. The new president, a well-respected musician and poet in Teresina, entered office and, suspecting foul play on the part of the previous president, promptly shut down the theater to evaluate how moneys were being used. After six difficult weeks of uncertainty about whether or not the Atelier would be defunded, which would force its members to seek out new forms of employment, the theater was reopened. Only this time, the Atelier's access to and involvement with it would be far more restricted. Under the new administration, the theater would be used mostly for local and largely traditional musical performances and children's events. For Yuri—who proposed the very idea for the theater's construction in this marginalized neighborhood—and the Atelier, this new arrangement felt like a slap in the face. Pedro explained that feeling both underappreciated and disrespected by the new powers-that-be, the Atelier was currently considering abandoning the theater all together. Some participants were already in the process of looking for a new space. The biggest concern, however, was that such a move would come at a great expense: it would mean everyone in the Atelier sacrificing their salaries, which for a good many would result in giving up performance art all together and looking for another minimum-wage job—for example, cleaning houses or driving buses—to enable them to continue contributing to their families' incomes.

When I asked Pedro and Luciana why they thought such a dramatic change was taking place at the theater, they said that while it was quite possible that the previous president had mismanaged funds, the more probable reason was that the new president was essentially kicking them out because of the kind of work they do. That is, their work challenged his concept of "culture." The new president, they told me, opposes anything he perceives to be contaminating traditional, local culture. Apparently, because Yuri established his career as a contemporary dancer, choreographer, and performance artist in Europe, and had forged an ongoing dialogue between the Atelier and artists abroad, the new president saw the Atelier's work as a European import, of little benefit to the city and state.

It initially surprised me that a person in charge of cultural events in Teresina could lack an appreciation for this group and its achievements. Since its inception, the Atelier has created original pieces that its members have performed at festivals throughout Brazil and in Europe and Asia, and it has brought numerous artists from abroad to Teresina to collaborate on projects. Moreover, the Atelier's work tends to be quite sophisticated—not only in terms of originality but also by way of social critique. Always a complex mixture of so-called local and foreign influences, the Atelier's work often calls into question a number of social and cultural conventions. But, Luciana and Pedro explained, the new president values none of that, only traditional music and folklore. Anything else is a foreign import, ultimately threatening the integrity of local culture. To make his position clear, they told me, during television interviews the president has apparently even pretended not to understand common Portuguese words appropriated from English (e.g., "email"). For Pedro and Luciana, the new president was a cultural purist who did not understand that culture is never homogenous, is always changing, and is, at its very essence, a dialogue between local and foreign ways of life. Seen this way, conforming to the new rules that the president had implemented would limit the Atelier's concept of culture, art, and freedom of expression. Two days after our conversation over lunch, the Atelier left the theater in solidarity with numerous artists and patrons in Teresina and beyond—an act of resistance that eventually became a performance piece of its own.

*   *   *

Considering the broader context, the new president's position seemed quite logical: as upwardly mobile Teresinenses reach for countless symbols of *fora* (outside worlds imagined to be superior) to land themselves *chique* (chic) status in their city, the new president feared the eradication of a discernable local culture. It made sense, then, that he would seek to cultivate and maintain a distinct cultural identity for the city and state in the hopes of claiming a place for both on the national map. The Atelier, while also concerned with recognition and establishing a sense of belonging, took up a radically different position from the new president as well as from Teresina's fora-centric, upwardly mobile mainstream society. Rather than relying on a notion of "culture" as fixed, in which the local and the foreign are bound and opposing cultural entities, or striving for recognition by appropriating symbols of fora, the Atelier positioned itself within a world of artists that is both local *and* cosmopolitan, forging a sense of belonging with a community that understands culture as "dialogue."

Though my portrayal of the conflict between the Atelier and the new president of the cultural foundation is likely an oversimplification of matters, the basic dynamic is reminiscent of a tendency that underpins much of what I have demonstrated in this book. That is, in a city like Teresina, which is increasingly connected to distant worlds, carving out a sense of belonging depends on inserting oneself and others into multiple discourses about space and time. For example, in Chap. 2, I illustrate how the concept of fora can make Teresina appear developmentally delayed in the face of a constellation of more advanced and distant worlds. And in Chap. 3, I show how engaging in performances of chique can help Teresinenses establish belonging due to chique's association with a more advanced quality of life and/or proximity to fora. Inherent in these chique performances is a move to distance oneself in both space and time from specific peoples and places, whether within Teresina or elsewhere.

In a similar vein, the conflict between the Atelier and the president positions the two parties involved as diametrically opposed to one another: one attempts to shut out fora in an effort to revive a devalued traditional local culture, and the other, lacking support from the dominant society, looks elsewhere within and beyond the nation for validation, as if to say, "if Teresina won't recognize us, at least Rio, Amsterdam, and Tokyo will." Following this interpretation, the president comes to stand in for the "local" and the Atelier for the "non-local/foreign/cosmopolitan." Such a polarization of these two positions is doubtless an exaggeration. Neither party is essentially one or the other—a fact that became glaringly apparent when I participated in part of a collaborative project sponsored by the Atelier.

Over the course of three weeks, I witnessed members of the Atelier engage in a number of activities that appeared extremely local in nature by involving residents and ways of life typical of the neighborhood—for example, speaking in the local vernacular, clapping one's hands rather than knocking on a resident's front door to get their attention, using moto-taxis to get around, and creating numerous artistic projects about traditional practices like the use of mule-drawn carts for transporting building materials, appliances, and trash. I had a similar realization when I accompanied a friend to an invitation-only performance of "La Casa de Bernarda Alba" (a Spanish play written by the famous Federico García Lorca) at a different theater with a different group of performers and observed the new president of the cultural foundation display extreme appreciation for this production rooted in the nonlocal.

As Tsing (2005) points out, such positioning of people and places within different geographical spaces (e.g., local and nonlocal/foreign) and times (e.g., behind and advanced) is simply an attempt to make meaning and to help people establish a sense of place and be-longing in the world at home. It is all a matter of perspective, for all it takes is digging deep enough in order to find that few things are truly "local," as most everything comes from somewhere else. I, too, have engaged in such positioning in writing this book about a particular place and people and their experience of be-longing. The spatial and temporal scales I have identified as meaningful in Teresina may be just as real or artificial as any other scales that help people make meaning of the worlds they inhabit. One of my goals, however, has been that this project allow readers to grasp the many ways that scales like "local," "fora," and "national" can be deployed around a place, and how they can coexist and be deployed in different ways and moments in the name of be-longing. In doing so, we begin to move further away from the increasingly problematic notion that we live in a world made up of decidedly "local" peoples and places on the one hand and "cosmopolitan/foreign" ones on the other.

*   *   *

From my portrayal of the Atelier, it should seem that there is a fair amount of overlap between this performance collective and the galera: not only are a handful of participants in the galera committed members of the Atelier, the two collectivities share a number of interests and perspectives on the world (e.g., experimentation, notions of the self and culture as fluid entities, and a general openness to and fascination with difference). That said, the two are also quite distinct. Being a member of the Atelier is akin to a full-time job and, as such, demands much sacrifice and commitment in terms of work and time. Members of the Atelier formulate projects and rehearse them for long hours during both day and night and cannot depend on forms of employment that restrict their ability to travel with their performances. Thus, members of the Atelier often live with far-fewer comforts than those commonly enjoyed by many participants in the galera; furthermore, members of the Atelier are overwhelmingly less embroiled than most galera participants in the task of negotiating the opposing worlds of nocturnal bohemia and normative daylife.

As Chaps. 4, 5, and 6 demonstrate, the galera, in contrast to the Atelier, operates through its own spatiotemporal matrix of belonging—one that is not entirely unlike another dynamic of spatiotemporality occurring in nature: the coral reef. Like the galera's nocturnal bohemia, coral reefs offer a place for a number of different types of organisms to not only take refuge but to thrive. Locations of refuge like coral reefs can be areas for cooling off or warming up or may simply provide the ideal conditions for particular populations to flourish. Havens of a rich diversity of life, coral reefs provide organisms that might otherwise perish the opportunity to prosper (Mulhall 2009). Also like a coral reef, the galera exists at once in relative isolation and in constant contact with the broader context in which it is steeped. Isolated enough to provide refuge, yet not separated from neighboring waters, organisms, and other elements, coral reefs and their surrounding environment mutually influence and cocreate one another.

With the metaphor of the coral reef, then, the galera's modes of operation are known processes for survival. And it seems that the flexible and dynamic nature of Teresina's galera is not only like that of coral reefs, but is also symptomatic of a larger process taking place in countless other cities throughout the world. As cities and new technologies expand at exponential rates, the world appears both smaller and larger than it did before. It is smaller in the sense that people can connect to peoples, places, and information that were not long ago little more than a figment of the imagination. Yet the world also looks bigger than ever when one considers the enormous physical reach of these peoples, places, and information that have become so integral to daily life. I think it is safe to say that in such a world, it is virtually impossible to have it all. That is to say, the distant worlds people imagine, feel an affinity for, and even sense an intimate connection with are far more numerous than those they are given the opportunity to physically travel to and experience firsthand. For places like Teresina, these changes are accompanied by something far more complex than a limitation: a way of life structured around creatively maneuvering in and out of differing contexts and geographic scales. A way of life that forges a sense of belonging, both in the world, and at home.

REFERENCES

Mulhall, Marjorie. 2009. Saving Rainforests of the Sea: An Analysis of International Efforts to Conserve Coral Reefs. *Duke Environmental Law and Policy Forum* 19: 321–351.

Tsing, Anna Lowenhaupt. 2005. *Friction: An Ethnography of Global Connections.* Princeton: Princeton University Press.

GLOSSARY OF PORTUGUESE TERMS

B-R-O; BRÓ Teresina's hottest, driest, and sunniest season of the year; it is named as such because it includes all of the months ending in "BRO"—that is, *setembro, outubro, novembro,* and *dezembro.*

Chique a term used to describe something extraordinarily beautiful, sophisticated, expensive, or simply impressive; it can point to virtually any person, place, or thing that is thought to be above and beyond the necessary, ordinary, or quotidian in Teresina.

Festa a party. Within the galera, the term usually refers to a highly produced dance-club type event that that charges admission and can take place in a variety of locales ranging from an abandoned residence or the grounds of a country house to a hall or a dance club.

Fora outside. Often used to refer to an imagined set of distant places and cultures thought to be culturally and economically superior, more developed, more progressive, whiter, and cooler in temperature.

Frei Serafim historically, Teresina's principal avenue, bisecting the city between North and South.

Galera clique: popularly used throughout Brazil to reference a loosely knit group of friends. The term is used throughout the book to refer to the clique of people who come together in Teresina's nocturnal bohemia.

GLS an acronym stemming from the LGBT movement in Brazil to institutionalize gay spaces as not exclusively "*Gay*" or "*Lesbica,*" but also "S," which stands for "*simpatizantes,*" meaning "sympathizers."

© The Author(s) 2019
T. E. Murphy, *Queerly Cosmopolitan,*
https://doi.org/10.1007/978-3-030-00296-1

Mafrense an in-group term appropriated by some participants in the galera to point to people attempting to appear chique while maintaining a life-style and outlook that is stereotypically local and parochial, ranging from small-minded and naive to close-minded, ignorant, and inconsiderate.

Nordestino a person from the Brazilian Northeast.

Ovelha negra black sheep.

Parnaíba the larger of the two rivers that intersect in Teresina, marking the border between the states Piauí and Maranhão.

Piauiense a person from the state of Piauí, of which Teresina is the capital.

Poti the smaller of the two rivers that intersect in Teresina.

Teresinense a person from the city of Teresina.

Referência reference. A term participants in the galera use to refer to the extent to which a person has an understanding of something—particularly a culture, aesthetic, event, or practice—that is imagined to exist in another (and often distant) place and time.

Index[1]

[1]Note: Page numbers followed by 'n' refer to notes.

© The Author(s) 2019

T. E. Murphy, *Queerly Cosmopolitan*,

https://doi.org/10.1007/978-3-030-00296-1

153

Foreign, 3, 9, 12, 14, 27n1, 35, 37,
  38, 48, 56n2, 65, 68, 69, 105,
  108, 114, 128, 145–148
Friendships, viii, 12, 135, 139
Furtado, C., 29, 30

G
Galera (clique)
  ethos of queerness, 14, 15, 76, 93,
    94, 111, 112, 136
  events, 79, 112, 136
  experimentation and novelty, 89–90
  nonnormativity, 14–16, 76
  relationship to bourgeois society,
    89, 91–93
  understandings of gender/sexuality,
    89, 135
Gender/sexuality
  alternative articulations of, 76
  competing understandings of,
    132–135
  experimentation with, 135
  nonnormative expressions of, 15, 90
  social class, 130
  socioeconomic status, 76
Globalization, 11–13
Green, J., 11
Green, S., 109

H
Halberstam, J., 15, 76, 77, 92, 136
Hannerz, U., 13
Heat
  backwardness, 27
  escaping, 55, 56
  extreme, 27, 28, 34, 37, 64
  inescapability of, 27
  poverty, 27, 38
  prevalence of, 26
  symbolism, 26, 27

I
Identification, 11, 14, 76, 77, 110, 139
Identity
  cultural, 146
  gender/sexual, 128, 133n5,
    135, 136
  public, 129, 135, 140
Imagination, 13, 75, 105, 106, 149
  cosmopolitan, 13, 106
Inequality, 8, 29, 30, 33
Inferiority, 9, 92
Innovation, 14, 81, 93, 114, 115, 117

K
Klinenberg, E., 27

L
Lack
  of culture, 9
  of importance, 9, 28, 35
  of resources, 9
Lause, M., 14, 15, 80, 89–91, 106, 107
Levi-Strauss, C., 26
LGBT
  community, 14, 76, 91, 136
  events and spaces, 15, 91, 139
  identity politics, 138
  movement, 15
Liechty, M., 13, 58
Lloyd, R., 15, 80, 93

M
Mafrense, 104–105, 111, 138
Marginality, 37
Margins
  of the globe, 12, 13
  of mainstream society, 14, 76,
    94, 136
McCullam, E., 76

CPSIA information can be obtained
at www.ICGtesting.com
Printed in the USA
LVHW010244291018
595162LV00013B/354/P

9 783030 002954